PROPS
PROVERBS & PSALMS APART
365 DAILY DEVOTIONS

MATTHEW MAHER

PROPS: PROVERBS & PSALMS APART

Copyright © 2025 by Matthew Maher. All rights reserved.

Edited by: Matthew Maher

This title is also available as a 55:11 Publishing product.

Visit www.truthovertrend.com/5511-publishing for more information.

Unless otherwise indicated, all materials on these pages are copyrighted by Matthew Maher. All rights reserved. No part of this publication may be reproduced, stored in an information or retrieval system, or transmitted in any form or by any means, electronic, mechanical, photocopying, recording, or otherwise, without the prior written permission of the Publisher, except as permitted by U.S. copyright law.

Scripture quotations are taken from the *New King James Version®*. Copyright © 1982 by Thomas Nelson. Used by permission. All rights reserved.

Published by:
55:11 Publishing LLC
1701 Walnut Street, 7th Floor
Philadelphia, Pennsylvania 19103 USA

5511publishing@gmail.com | www.truthovertrend.com/5511-publishing

55:11 Publishing is committed to Publishing with Purpose. The company reflects the philosophy established by the founders, based on Isaiah 55:11:

"So shall My word be that goes forth from My mouth; it shall not return to Me void, but it shall accomplish what I please, and it shall prosper in the thing for which I sent it."

Book design copyright © 2025 by 55:11 Publishing LLC. All rights reserved.

Cover design by: Polymer, www.HelloPolymer.com

Interior design by: Joanna Sanders LLC, www.colossians16.com

Published in the United States of America

ISBN (Paperback): 979-8-9911397-1-7

PROPS
PROVERBS & PSALMS APART
365 DAILY DEVOTIONS

MATTHEW MAHER

In Christ alone.

A special thanks to Joanna Sanders for her time and talent with this project.

✝

In honor of Hort Kap.

contents

Preface 1

Part I: Salvation 9

Part II: Understanding 57

Part III: Praise 107

Part IV: Perserverance 153

Part V: Opportunity 205

Part VI: Restoration 255

Part VII: Thankfulness 303

Nothing New Under the Sun 351

Epilogue 393

PREFACE

According to Merriam-Webster's Dictionary:

prop (noun)
1. something that props or sustains: support

prop (verb)
1. to support by placing something under or against—often used with up ("prop up")
2. sustain, strengthen, stabilize

According to Matthew Maher's Core Convictionary:

ProPs (pro + ps)
1. a combination of Proverbs and Psalms: two books that stabilize the soul and steady the heart.
2. support that offers—
    - **S**alvation
    - **U**nderstanding
    - **P**raise
    - **P**erseverance
    - **O**pportunity
    - **R**estoration
    - **T**hankfulness

What props you up on your leaning side?

Like the kickstand on a bike, the Proverbs and Psalms in the Bible act as stabilizers, keeping us upright and balanced no matter the terrain—whether we face rocky ground, sandy traps, or grassy meadows. Even those who don't believe the Bible often recognize the Psalms and Proverbs. There's something universal about these books that steadies the soul, offering a sense of balance before life demands we pedal forward again.

To me, the Proverbs represent *"core convictions"*—timeless truths and divine principles that God calls us to heed if we are to live wisely and faithfully. They are short sayings with long meanings, offering clarity and strength when life's demands feel overwhelming. Psalms, on the other hand, reflect the raw emotions of humanity—ranging from cries of despair to songs of celebration. They remind us that God meets us in the highs and lows. Both books sustain and guide us, propping us up on our leaning side when life threatens to knock us down.

There's a reason these two books are among the most quoted and cherished parts of Scripture. Their brevity makes them accessible, but it's their honesty and realness that make them unforgettable. Even skeptics recognize the wisdom and comfort found in their words.

It was with this shared appreciation that I set out to combine the truths and treasures of these "kickstands" into one devotional. This 365-day journey highlights selected Proverbs and Psalms—what I call ***"ProPs"***—to help us navigate the unpredictable paths of life. We don't know what the road ahead holds, but we do know Who holds the road.

The Contemplate & Cultivate Approach

Each verse in this devotional is explored twice, across two parts: one day to reflect, one day to respond. That's the rhythm. **Contemplate** invites you to slow down and wrestle with the truth; **Cultivate** calls you to apply it, let it take root, and walk it out. That rhythm of renewal shaped my own spiritual journey behind prison walls, and it forms the heartbeat of this devotional.

Proverbs 3:5–6 isn't just tattooed on my arm—it's engraved on the tablet of my heart: *"Trust in the Lord with all your heart, and lean not on your own understanding; in all your ways acknowledge Him, and He shall direct your paths."* That truth steadied me when the road got rocky, the path was unclear, or the weight was too much to bear. And even when I was sinking in the mess of my own making, God's Word became my kickstand.

When we lean into divine truth, we find our footing. Trusting God's Word instead of our own perspective allows Him to direct every step. These *ProPs* are spiritual support beams, sustaining us when life shakes beneath us—whether in valleys, on mountaintops, or navigating sharp turns. His strength will always sustain.

Through the timeless wisdom of the Proverbs and the raw honesty of the Psalms, we discover truths that steady us in life's trials. Though circumstances shift, God remains the same yesterday, today, and forever (Hebrews 13:8). His Word alone sustains, maintains, and remains.

Take time to drink deeply from these *Proverbs and Psalms Apart*, and you will find them as nourishing and strengthening as I have. The passages I share in this devotional are those that profoundly impacted my soul and fortified my faith during my time of confinement. I do not boast in my circumstances; rather, I boast in the One who carried me through them.

His grace became my kickstand in the unstable soil of incarceration—and it can be the same for you. No matter where you are, His strength is made perfect in your weakness (2 Corinthians 12:9). Trust Him to uphold you, to steady your leaning side, and to keep you moving forward in faith.

That's why this devotional leans into what I call the *"Biblical Equation of ProPs."*

The Biblical Equation of ProPs:
Proverbs + Psalms = ProPs!

One offers God's wisdom; the other offers our worship. Proverbs gives us divine instruction for daily living: principles of wisdom, integrity, and discipline that help us walk uprightly in a fallen world. Psalms gives voice to our human condition: raw and real prayers that remind us God is near in every season, from the pit to the praise. Together, they balance us. When meditated upon, they work like a spiritual equation that produces godly results: Proverbs guides our choices; Psalms shapes our response. Head and heart. Truth and trust. Instruction and intimacy. That's the stabilizing power of *ProPs*.

But there's more, because when Christ becomes the common denominator in this equation, everything changes. He bridges the gap between our human imperfections and God's perfect standard. With Proverbs and Psalms as the foundation and Christ at the center, our lives become balanced, strengthened, and upheld, no matter how unpredictable the world around us may be.

The Beginning of Proverbs:
To know wisdom and instruction, to perceive the words of understanding, to receive the instruction of wisdom, justice, judgment, and equity; to give prudence to the simple, to the young man knowledge and discretion—A wise man will hear and increase learning, and a man of understanding will attain wise counsel, to understand a Proverb and an enigma, the words of the wise and their riddles. (Proverbs 1:2-6)

The Beginning of Psalms:
Blessed is the man who walks not in the counsel of the ungodly, nor stands in the path of sinners, nor sits in the seat of the scornful, but his delight is in the law of the Lord, and in His law he meditates day and night. He shall be like a tree planted by the rivers of water, that brings forth its fruit in its season, whose leaf also shall not wither; and whatever he does shall prosper. (Psalm 1:1-3)

Taken together, Proverbs and Psalms give us a full picture of how to walk with God daily — both in our actions and our affections.

Proverbs focus on *practical living*.
Psalms focus on the *practice of praise*.

Proverbs are to be *contemplated for action*.
Psalms are to be *contemplated for reflection*.

Proverbs speak *from man to man*.
Psalms speak *from man to God*.

Proverbs engage the *mind for growth*.
Psalms engage the *spirit for depth*.

Proverbs guide our *public walk*.
Psalms guide our *private worship*.

Proverbs *sharpen our wisdom*.
Psalms *shape our worship*.

Proverbs teach us how to *walk before men*.
Psalms teach us how to *kneel before God*.

Proverbs train our *hands for life*.
Psalms train our *hearts for God*.

Together, Proverbs and Psalms provide both direction and devotion, instruction and intimacy, wisdom and worship—equipping us to live fully for God.

PART I

SALVATION

Proverbs & Psalms That Help, Deliver, And Save:
The SUPPORT That Pulls Your Head
Above The Water!

JANUARY 1

Salvation belongs to the Lord. Your blessing is upon Your people. (Psalm 3:8)

Contemplate → The Hebrew word for salvation can mean *"having room to breathe."* When we acknowledge that salvation belongs to the Lord and accept His saving grace, He frees us from the suffocating grip of our circumstances. The very root of the word "salvation" is "Yeshua," the very name of Jesus—the One who gives us the breath of life.

How often do we let the weight of life steal the very breath we need to thrive? This Psalm reminds us that God's salvation restores the life-giving oxygen our souls desperately need. His blessings deliver us, lifting our heads above the waters of despair and giving us room to breathe.

Are you gasping for air in life's struggles? In this new year, it's time to turn to the One who offers true deliverance, for His salvation alone provides the breath of life.

†

JANUARY 2

Salvation belongs to the Lord. Your blessing is upon Your people. (Psalm 3:8)

Cultivate → Yesterday, we reflected on how God's salvation gives us *room to breathe*—freeing us from the suffocating weight of circumstances. But salvation is not just about rescue; it's about *renewal.* God doesn't just pull us out of the water—He teaches us how to swim. Today, let's cultivate this truth in our hearts and lives.

Where in your life do you feel like you're gasping for air? Is there an area where you've been trying to "save yourself" instead of resting in God's deliverance? Every time you feel overwhelmed today, pause and take a deep breath. As you inhale, silently say, *"Salvation belongs to the Lord."* As you exhale, pray, *"Your blessing is upon Your people."* Let this simple rhythm train your heart to rest in His provision.

Salvation is not just a moment; it's a lifestyle of trust. Cultivate the habit of breathing in God's presence today.

†

JANUARY 3

Every word of God is pure; He is a shield to those who put their trust in Him. (Proverbs 30:5)

Contemplate → God's Word is flawless, untainted by error or deceit, because it flows from His perfect character. His promises are tested and true, refined like the purest silver. When you trust in Him and His Word, He becomes your shield—a protector in life's battles, guarding your heart, mind, and soul.

The word *shield* appears over seventy times in the Bible, often symbolizing God's protection. In ancient warfare, shields were often linked together to create a protective wall—each shield reinforcing the next. This reflects how faith works in community. When you trust God's Word alongside other believers, you strengthen one another against the enemy's attacks (Ephesians 6:16).

Faith flourishes in fellowship, where the shields of others strengthen our own in moments of weakness. This doesn't mean trials won't come, but His shield ensures victory. Though storms may rage and attacks arise, His truth remains unshaken, fortifying every weak side. Stand firm behind His shield and trust in His pure Word, knowing He never fails His people.

†

JANUARY 4

Every word of God is pure; He is a shield to those who put their trust in Him. (Proverbs 30:5)

Cultivate → Trust is only as strong as the foundation it rests on. God's Word is pure, and His protection is sure, but a shield only works if we stand behind it. Too often, we rely on our own strength instead of trusting Him fully.

Where are you struggling to trust the Lord? What burdens from last year can you surrender? Trusting God isn't weakness—it's wisdom. Identify those areas and pray this or write your own:

"Lord, thank You for Your pure Word and faithful protection. I surrender my fears and choose to stand behind Your shield. Teach me to trust You fully. Amen."

Today, when fear or worry creeps in, remind yourself: *God's Word is pure. His shield is strong. I will trust in Him.*

†

JANUARY 5

He shall be like a tree planted by the rivers of water, that brings forth its fruit in its season, whose leaf also shall not wither; and whatever he does shall prosper.
(Psalm 1:3)

Contemplate → A tree's strength isn't found in its size but in its roots. It doesn't struggle to bear fruit—it simply stays planted where nourishment is abundant. Likewise, when we delight in God's Word, we are firmly anchored, drawing life from Him in every season.

The *rivers of water* represent the constant flow of God's truth, sustaining us through both drought and storm. Deep roots grow strongest during dry seasons, as they push further into the soil in search of water. In the same way, our faith matures most when we rely on God's Word in difficult times.

We may not always see immediate growth, but in the right season, we will bear fruit. The promise is not a life free of hardship, but a life preserved and flourishing in what truly matters.

Consider the mangrove tree, thriving where tides shift and soil is salty. Its strength isn't in escaping difficulty, but in sending its roots deep and wide to anchor itself amid the chaos. In a similar way, our lives—rooted in

God's Word—can remain stable even when everything around us changes.

Are you staying rooted in His Word daily? The depth of your roots determines the strength of your faith and the fruit you bear.

†

JANUARY 6

He shall be like a tree planted by the rivers of water, that brings forth its fruit in its season, whose leaf also shall not wither; and whatever he does shall prosper.
(Psalm 1:3)

Cultivate → Being rooted in God's Word nourishes and sustains us through every season. Just as a tree draws life from deep waters, our souls thrive when we soak in His truth. But roots must grow before fruit appears—strength comes through abiding. A tree doesn't bear fruit overnight; it flourishes through steady growth, remaining connected to its source.

Write down a verse that refreshes your soul. Reflect on how it has nourished you in different seasons and strengthened your faith. Keep it somewhere visible as a daily reminder that just as a tree thrives by a river, your soul flourishes in God's Word. And remember, *root determines fruit*—the deeper your roots in Christ, the more abundant the harvest.

"Lord, help me remain rooted in Your Word, drawing my strength from You in every season. Let my life bear fruit that reflects Your truth, and may I stand firm like a tree planted by Your waters. Amen."

†

JANUARY 7

There are many plans in a man's heart, nevertheless the Lord's counsel—that will stand. (Proverbs 19:21)

Contemplate → Our hearts are often filled with ambitions and plans, but unless they align with God's will, they are destined to falter. This Proverb reminds us that only the Lord's counsel is unshakable—unchanging in the face of uncertainty, unwavering despite human efforts.

When we submit our plans to His purpose, we find true success—not as the world defines it, but as God ordains it. His wisdom sees beyond what we can comprehend, guiding us toward what is best rather than what is merely good. The foundation of His counsel will stand through every trial and uncertainty.

Trust Him to direct your steps, and you will walk firmly in His way, knowing His plans are always greater than our own.

†

JANUARY 8

There are many plans in a man's heart, nevertheless the Lord's counsel—that will stand. (Proverbs 19:21)

Cultivate → Plans may shift, but God's counsel remains firm. While we carefully map out our steps, wisdom calls us to seek His direction above our own. Have you sought His counsel for the situations you face today? It's easy to rely on our own understanding, but true peace comes when we submit our plans to Him. The more we align with His will, the less we wrestle with uncertainty. His wisdom outlasts every fleeting idea or temporary solution we may create.

Take a moment now to pause and pray: *"Lord, align my heart with Your will. Let my decisions be guided by Your counsel, not my own desires. Help me to trust in Your greater plan, even when I don't fully understand it."*

Throughout the day, when you feel uncertain, remind yourself: *My plans may change, but God's counsel will stand.* Walk in that assurance today, knowing that His wisdom never fails.

†

JANUARY 9

He is my rock and my salvation; He is my defense; I shall not be moved. (Psalm 62:6)

Contemplate → Nothing in this world provides the stability and security of the Rock of Ages. David boldly declares, *"I shall not be moved,"* because God alone is his salvation and defense. This is not a mere wish—it's a proclamation of trust in God's unchanging nature.

When life's storms rage, the one anchored in Christ remains immovable. A rock withstands the fiercest winds without shifting, and so will we when God is our foundation. His strength is not dependent on circumstances, and His promises do not waver under pressure.

Let your heart echo this truth: *He alone. He is. I shall not be moved.*

†

JANUARY 10

He is my rock and my salvation; He is my defense; I shall not be moved. (Psalm 62:6)

Cultivate → Security isn't found in the absence of storms but in the strength of your foundation. God is our Rock and defense, but declaring, *"I shall not be moved,"* isn't just a statement—it's a stance. Storms will come, and when they do, where you stand determines whether you'll be shaken.

What storm is tossing you to and fro right now? The situation may feel unstable, but your foundation doesn't have to be. Stability isn't found in circumstances—it's found in Christ. Take a moment to stand firm in faith. Look your storm in the eye and declare with David: *"I shall not be moved."*

Throughout the day, remind yourself: *My hope is not in shifting sands. My feet are planted on the Rock of Ages.* Hold onto this truth, no matter what winds may blow.

"Lord, when the storms rage around me, keep my feet steady on Your unshakable foundation. Let my faith stand firm in Your salvation. Amen."

†

JANUARY 11

Blessed is the man who listens to me, watching daily at my gates, waiting at the posts of my door. For whoever finds me finds life, and obtains favor from the Lord.
(Proverbs 8:34-35)

Contemplate → There is no greater pursuit than the pursuit of wisdom. But wisdom isn't merely an abstract idea—it is a person. Scripture tells us that, *"Christ Jesus . . . became for us wisdom from God"* (1 Corinthians 1:30). To listen to wisdom is to listen to Him.

The gates in this Proverb symbolize places where decisions were made, justice was given, and important matters were discussed. In ancient Israel, city gates functioned as a community hub where elders provided counsel and leaders made crucial choices. Likewise, when we seek Christ's wisdom, we are equipping ourselves for life's defining moments.

Wisdom does not come to the passive—it is found by those who watch daily and wait expectantly. Are you positioning yourself to hear His voice? To listen is to discern. To wait is to prepare. And to find wisdom is to find Christ, Himself.

†

JANUARY 12

Blessed is the man who listens to me, watching daily at my gates, waiting at the posts of my door. For whoever finds me finds life, and obtains favor from the Lord.
(Proverbs 8:34-35)

Cultivate → Maybe you've been asking, but are you listening? Seeking wisdom isn't just about presenting our questions to God—it's about being attentive to His answers. Wisdom calls out, but do we pause long enough to hear?

Identify one area where you need wisdom today. Is it a decision weighing on you? A conversation you're unsure how to navigate? A struggle where clarity seems distant? Bring it before God, but don't rush away. Spend a moment in stillness, asking Him for guidance, and remain watchful for His direction throughout your day.

As you reflect, ask God, *"What are You teaching me in this season?"* Write down any impressions or Scriptures that come to mind. Jot down any insights, Scriptures, or nudges you sense from Him. As you listen, remember: *Blessing follows those who wait at wisdom's door.*

†

JANUARY 13

They confronted me in the day of my calamity, but the Lord was my support. (Psalm 18:18)

Contemplate → Adversity often reveals who is truly on our side. In the *day of calamity,* when we are most vulnerable, the enemy seizes the opportunity to strike. Hardships have a way of exposing where our trust lies and who we rely on when everything feels uncertain.

Yet, this verse assures us that even when we are surrounded by opposition, God's support keeps us upright. He upholds us when others fail us, giving us strength to endure and overcome. His presence is not conditional, nor is His faithfulness dependent on our circumstances.

The storms of life may confront us, but we are not defeated, for the Lord is our unfailing support in every trial.

†

JANUARY 14

They confronted me in the day of my calamity, but the Lord was my support. (Psalm 18:18)

Cultivate → Trials have a way of exposing where our trust truly lies. When calamity strikes, do we lean on our own strength, or do we rest in the support of the Lord?

Consider a past or present trial in your life. How did—or how does—God uphold you? Take a moment to reflect on His provision, whether through His Word, His peace, or His people. If you're in the midst of difficulty, lift a prayer of trust. If He has already brought you through, offer a prayer of gratitude.

"Lord, even when adversity surrounds me, I trust in You to uphold me. Thank You for being my constant support in every trial. Help me stand firm, knowing You will never fail me. Amen."

Let this truth settle in your heart today: *Storms may come, but my support will not fail, for the Lord is with me.*

†

JANUARY 15

The fruit of the righteous is a tree of life, and he who wins souls is wise. (Proverbs 11:30)

Contemplate → Adam and Eve lost access to the tree of life because of their disobedience, plunging humanity into a fallen state. Yet, through Jesus Christ's redeeming work on the cross, access to the tree of life is restored for all who believe. In Him, we are no longer bound by the curse of sin but are made alive to bear fruit that lasts.

In Hebrew thought, the "tree of life" symbolized strength, stability, and continual fruitfulness. In Christ, we are called to bear fruit that nourishes those around us—not merely for our own growth, but to reflect the eternal life He offers.

Winning souls for Christ is the ultimate act of wisdom because it leads others to eternal life. Is your life producing the kind of fruit that draws others closer to Jesus? Salvation is not meant to stop with us; it is meant to flow through us to a world desperate for hope.

†

JANUARY 16

The fruit of the righteous is a tree of life, and he who wins souls is wise. (Proverbs 11:30)

Cultivate → A life rooted in Christ bears fruit that nourishes others. Just as a tree provides shade, strength, and sustenance, the fruit of righteousness brings life to those around us. But fruit isn't meant to stay on the branch—it's meant to be shared.

Write down the name of someone who needs encouragement or the truth of the gospel. Reach out to them with a message, a call, or a simple reminder that they are loved. Remember, fruit doesn't appear overnight. Sometimes the seeds you sow may seem unseen, but trust that God is growing something beautiful in His time. Don't delay!

"Lord, open my eyes to those around me who need Your truth. Give me boldness to share, wisdom to speak, and love that reflects Your heart. Use me to bear fruit that leads others to You. Amen."

†

JANUARY 17

Let integrity and uprightness preserve me, for I wait for You. (Proverbs 25:21)

Contemplate → Salvation is not only about deliverance; it's also about preservation. God doesn't just rescue us—He sustains us. This verse reminds us that integrity and uprightness act as anchors, keeping us steady as we wait for His perfect timing.

How we conduct ourselves when no one is watching is a testament to the strength of our faith. The waiting season is not wasted; it is where God refines us. While waiting for Him to act, we don't sit idly—we continue to live in obedience, trusting that He will preserve us in the process.

Victory often begins in the quiet moments of faithfulness before God brings the breakthrough. Are you remaining steadfast while you wait?

†

JANUARY 18

Let integrity and uprightness preserve me, for I wait for You. (Proverbs 25:21)

Cultivate → Integrity isn't just about doing the right thing—it's about being the same person in private as in public. It's a heart anchored in truth, unwavering despite circumstances.

We are all a work in progress, but growth requires reflection. In what areas do you need to realign your heart to better reflect a life fully devoted to God? Are there habits, thoughts, or compromises that need surrendering? Ask God to refine your integrity so that both your private and public life reflect His righteousness.

"Lord, shape my heart to walk in integrity before You. Help me remain steadfast in faith, whether seen or unseen, and trust that You are preserving me as I wait on You. Amen."

Walk today with a heart whole before God, knowing that integrity isn't just what you do—it's who you are in Him.

†

JANUARY 19

Trust in the Lord with all your heart, and lean not on your own understanding; in all your ways acknowledge Him, and He shall direct your paths. (Proverbs 3:5-6)

Contemplate → This is my life verse, given to me by my mother when I was a child. It has held me together through difficult times.

Trusting in God requires surrendering our limited understanding and placing full confidence in His infinite wisdom. When we rely on our own reasoning, we are bound to stumble. But when we acknowledge God in every aspect of life, He transforms even the most crooked paths into straight ones.

Think of God's Spirit like a spiritual GPS—calmly recalculating when we veer off course, never panicking, never giving up. He doesn't abandon us for making a wrong turn; He lovingly redirects us back toward the path of peace.

Through my own trials, I've learned that leaning on God makes the difference between falling apart and standing firm. He is the architect of clarity and the one who makes rough roads smooth. *Trust in the Lord!*

†

JANUARY 20

Trust in the Lord with all your heart, and lean not on your own understanding; in all your ways acknowledge Him, and He shall direct your paths. (Proverbs 3:5-6)

Cultivate → Trusting God isn't passive—it's an intentional act of surrender. Too often, we lean on our own understanding, trying to control outcomes instead of releasing them to Him. But true peace comes when we acknowledge God in every step and trust Him to make the way clear.

Think about one area where you've been relying on your own reasoning. Surrender it to God in prayer, asking Him to lead you. As you seek Him, be still and listen—what is He revealing to you? Jot down any insights or Scriptures He brings to mind.

"Lord, I release my need for control and place this situation in Your hands. Direct my steps and align my heart with Your wisdom. I trust You completely. Amen."

Walk today with confidence, knowing that when you trust Him fully, He will guide you faithfully.

†

JANUARY 21

He sent His word and healed them, and delivered them from their destructions. (Psalm 107:20)

Contemplate → God's ultimate act of healing came when He sent His Son, Jesus, the living Word, into the world. As John 1:1-2 declares, *"In the beginning was the Word (Jesus), and the Word was with God, and the Word was God."* Through His written Word (logos), through His spoken Word (rhema), and through His living Word (Jesus), God provides healing and deliverance for all who turn to Him.

The sickness of sin has ravaged humanity, leaving brokenness in its wake. But by hiding God's Word in our hearts and embracing Christ as our Savior, we are rescued from destruction. His Word does not merely inform—it transforms.

His Word is not just a message; it is the power of life and salvation for all who believe. Have you allowed His Word to bring healing and restoration into your life?

†

JANUARY 22

He sent His word and healed them, and delivered them from their destructions. (Psalm 107:20)

Cultivate → Yesterday, we reflected on how God's Word is more than just words on a page—it is *living, powerful, and able to heal and deliver.* His Word doesn't just inform; it transforms.

This does not mean we will all be healed of infirmities. But it does mean that He is in the act of delivering us toward deeper reliance on Him. No matter what you are suffering, trust that His presence is your refuge.

Commit this verse to memory today: *"He sent His word and healed them, and delivered them from their destructions."* Write it on a note card or type it in your phone as a reminder that His Word still heals and delivers today.

"Lord, thank You for the healing and deliverance You have brought into my life. Your Word has restored me, guided me, and saved me. Help me to trust in its power daily. Amen."

†

JANUARY 23

Cast your burden on the Lord, and He shall sustain you; He shall never permit the righteous to be moved. (Psalm 55:22)

Contemplate → To *cast* means to release, to throw away, to discard. You cannot say you've cast something unless it has left your possession. This Psalm instructs us to release our burdens to God, not just acknowledge them.

A burden is anything weighing us down, preventing us from breathing freely. That's why one meaning of *salvation* is *"room to breathe,"* and another is *"preservation."* When we cast our burdens on the Lord, He promises to sustain us and preserve us.

This is the only solution when life feels heavy and overwhelming. If we truly release our burdens to God, He will keep us light, sustaining us in His presence.

What weight do you need to let go of today?

†

JANUARY 24

Cast your burden on the Lord, and He shall sustain you; He shall never permit the righteous to be moved. (Psalm 55:22)

Cultivate → Yesterday, we reflected on what it truly means to cast our burdens—to fully release them into God's hands. But letting go is often the hardest part. We may pray about our burdens, yet still carry them as if God needs our help to fix them.

What is weighing you down today? Identify one burden, write it down, and pray over it. Then, as an act of trust, symbolically cast it onto the Lord—tear up the paper, throw it away, or simply open your hands in surrender.

"Lord, I release this burden to You. I trust You to sustain me, to preserve me, and to keep me steady. Thank You for carrying what I was never meant to bear. Amen."

Once you release your burden, leave it with Him. If you're tempted to pick it back up, remind yourself: *I have cast this onto the Lord—He will sustain me.*

†

JANUARY 25

The horse is prepared for the day of battle, but deliverance is of the Lord. (Proverbs 21:31)

Contemplate → Preparation is vital—this Proverb acknowledges the effort we must put into readiness. We are called to plan, equip ourselves, and be diligent. However, this verse reminds us that the ultimate deliverance comes from God.

No matter how much we prepare, success is not in our hands but in His. Battles in life require both diligence and dependence. We must be ready, sharpen our skills, and face the fight with courage, but never forget that victory belongs to the Lord. True wisdom understands that preparation is our responsibility, but the outcome is always in His sovereign control.

He alone turns preparation into triumph, ensuring the outcome aligns with His perfect will. The question is: Are you trusting more in your preparation or in His power? Let every effort be surrendered to the One who holds the final victory.

†

JANUARY 26

The horse is prepared for the day of battle, but deliverance is of the Lord. (Proverbs 21:31)

Cultivate → Readiness is wise, but trust determines the outcome. We can train, plan, and equip ourselves for what lies ahead, yet victory is ultimately in God's hands. The challenge isn't just in preparing but in surrendering the outcome to Him.

Are you placing more confidence in your own efforts than in God's power? Take a moment to commit your plans to Him. Ask for wisdom to prepare well, but also the faith to release the results into His hands.

"Lord, I will be diligent in what You've called me to do, but I trust You with the outcome. Strengthen my heart to walk in faith, knowing You hold the victory. Amen."

Move forward today with both readiness and reliance—giving your best while trusting God for the rest.

†

JANUARY 27

I will lift up my eyes to the hills—from whence comes my help? My help comes from the Lord, Who made heaven and earth. (Psalm 121:1-2)

Contemplate → This simple yet powerful verse reminds us that *God is always ready to help those who seek Him.* He, the Creator of the universe, is fully capable of sustaining us in *all* circumstances.

This Psalm is a song of trust, where *lifting our eyes to the hills* can only be done from the valley. When we look upward to God—not backward at our regrets or forward in anxiety—we activate our faith, positioning ourselves to receive His help.

Notice that the Psalmist doesn't focus on the obstacles in his path but chooses to look up to the One who created and controls all things. *"Help comes from the Lord,"* and as our eyes look up, His provision and protection come down. Where is your focus today?

†

JANUARY 28

I will lift up my eyes to the hills—from whence comes my help? My help comes from the Lord, Who made heaven and earth. (Psalm 121:1-2)

Cultivate → It is in the valley that we desperately look for God's help. And it is there that we learn of His magnificent and faithful nature. The best way to enhance this miraculous intervention in our lives is to lift our eyes for someone else.

Help is not just something we receive—it's something we extend. Just as God is our ever-present Helper, we are called to reflect His love by encouraging others.

Write down the name of someone who may be struggling and set a reminder to check in with them today. A simple, intentional act of care can be the very encouragement they need to lift their eyes to the Lord.

"Lord, thank You for being my Helper in every season. Use me today to reflect Your love and encouragement to someone who needs it. Amen."

Be intentional today—your words may be the reminder someone needs to lift their eyes to Him.

†

JANUARY 29

Blessed be the Lord, Who daily loads us with benefits, the God of our salvation. (Psalm 68:19)

Contemplate → Just as we seek rewards for our labor, God generously loads us with daily benefits. These aren't merely material blessings but spiritual provisions that sustain our hearts and minds.

Unlike human employers who offer benefits in limited doses, God's grace, mercy, and joy are continuous, filling us daily. While employers may limit your vacation days or bonuses, God's grace has no cutoff point—His benefits are loaded upon you daily, without restriction or reservation. His benefits are weightless to us—free of stress and burdens—offering peace, hope, and strength.

As we cast our cares upon Him, He replaces them with His goodness. Let this Psalm encourage you to remember that God is the Everlasting Provider, offering daily renewal and blessings beyond what we can imagine.

†

JANUARY 30

Blessed be the Lord, Who daily loads us with benefits, the God of our salvation. (Psalm 68:19)

Cultivate → It is easy to overlook the countless ways God provides for us each day. His blessings, both seen and unseen, sustain us far beyond what we recognize in the moment.

Take time to intentionally reflect on His goodness. Write down three *"benefits"* God has provided for you today—whether spiritual, emotional, or physical. Consider how His daily provision strengthens and renews you. Then, spend a moment in gratitude, thanking Him for His abundant care.

"Lord, open my eyes to the blessings You pour into my life each day. Help me to recognize and appreciate Your faithful provision. Amen."

†

JANUARY 31

For You, O Lord, will bless the righteous; With favor You will surround him with a shield. (Psalm 5:12)

Contemplate → This is a bold declaration of the favor God extends to His people. When we are in Christ, we are surrounded by His grace like a shield. His blessings aren't uncertain or based on merit; they are guaranteed for the righteous.

We often ask God for just a favor, but He desires to give us *His* favor—and He surrounds us with it, offering protection and strength. So when people tell you that you are "hiding behind the Bible," embrace that truth! The Bible is our shield, our refuge, and our source of salvation.

The shield of God's favor is both defensive and offensive. It guards us from harm, but it also empowers us to step forward in faith, advancing in His strength. His favor goes before us like a shield in battle, guarding us from harm and guiding us with His love. Rejoice in this salvation today, knowing that you are surrounded by God's grace.

†

FEBRUARY 1

For You, O Lord, will bless the righteous; With favor You will surround him with a shield. (Psalm 5:12)

Cultivate → Remember, God's favor is a shield that *guards* and *guides*. His blessings aren't earned; they flow from His grace, surrounding us with His protection. His favor is not always seen in immediate ways, but when we look back, we can recognize how He has shielded us in ways we never expected.

Take a moment to reflect: Can you think of one specific area in which He has not only shown you favor but also clearly protected you? Consider how His presence has gone before you, shielding you from harm or guiding you through difficulty. Now, take that memory and use it as momentum to step forward in greater faith.

"Lord, thank You for surrounding me with Your favor. Help me to recognize Your protection in my life and trust in the shield of Your grace. Let me walk confidently, knowing You are my defender and my guide. Amen."

†

FEBRUARY 2

There is a way that seems right to a man, but its end is the way of death. (Proverbs 14:12)

Contemplate → This proverb unveils a harsh truth: what seems right in our own eyes can lead to destruction. Human wisdom, unrooted in God's truth, often deceives us into thinking we're on the right path. The world constantly offers paths that appear fulfilling—paths of self-reliance, success, or pleasure—but apart from God, they lead to emptiness and ruin.

Jesus is clear in John 14:6—*He is the Way, the Truth, and the Life.* True life is found only by following Christ, not our own desires. His way may not always seem easiest, but it is the only one that leads to true fulfillment and eternal life.

Take a moment to examine your path. If it's based solely on your perception and not God's Word, heed the warning of this proverb. There's still time to turn toward the Way that leads to life—His arms are always open, ready to guide you.

†

FEBRUARY 3

There is a way that seems right to a man, but its end is the way of death. (Proverbs 14:12)

Cultivate → Deception is dangerous because it feels true. Many have walked roads they were convinced were right, only to find destruction waiting at the end. The safeguard against deception is discernment—aligning our choices with God's Word rather than our emotions or culture's influence.

Today, test your direction by measuring it against Scripture. Choose one key decision you are facing and search the Bible for wisdom on the matter. Since deception often disguises itself as truth, ask God to reveal anything in your life that may seem right but is leading you away from Him. Let God's Word—not personal reasoning—confirm the steps you should take.

"Lord, I don't want to trust in what seems right—I want to follow what is right. Give me discernment to walk in Your way, to know Your truth, and to reflect Your life. Amen."

†

FEBRUARY 4

The Lord is my shepherd; I shall not want. He makes me to lie down in green pastures; He leads me beside the still waters. (Psalm 23:1-2)

Contemplate → Sheep are often seen as helpless animals—they wander, get lost, and sometimes even walk off cliffs. Yet David compares himself (and us) to sheep, not because he views himself as foolish, but because he humbly acknowledges his need for guidance and protection.

When the Lord is our Shepherd, we lack nothing. He will provide, protect, and prepare us, giving us exactly what He knows we need. He knows we need rest, so He *"makes me lie down in green pastures."* It's hard for a sheep to lie down when there's so much food to eat, yet the Shepherd gently guides them to rest, because they (and we) are easily disturbed.

By the Shepherd's comfort, the sheep can lie down and rest, knowing that provision surrounds them.

†

FEBRUARY 5

The Lord is my shepherd; I shall not want. He makes me to lie down in green pastures; He leads me beside the still waters. (Psalm 23:1-2)

Cultivate → The Shepherd knows exactly what His sheep need, leading them *beside still waters* because He understands their fears. Sheep are easily startled, hesitant to drink from rushing streams. In the same way, God doesn't push us into overwhelming places—He guides us to peace, refreshing us with His living water.

Take a moment today to slow down and rest in His care. Set aside five minutes of stillness—no distractions, no agenda—just time to be quiet before the Lord. Let His presence refresh you as you remember that He leads, provides, and protects.

"Lord, thank You for being my Shepherd, providing for my needs and leading me to places of rest and refreshment. Help me trust Your guidance and find peace in Your care. Amen."

†

FEBRUARY 6

He restores my soul; He leads me in the paths of righteousness for His name's sake. (Psalm 23:3)

Contemplate → The gentle voice and touch of the Shepherd restores our souls through His peace, which guards our hearts and minds. His restoration is not just about healing from past wounds, but about continual renewal—strengthening us daily so we can walk forward with confidence.

The soul is the heart of our emotions, and often our emotions are scattered, like lost sheep. Fear, doubt, and weariness can pull us in different directions, but only God's voice and touch can restore, bring back, and build us up. He doesn't just mend brokenness—He revives, refreshes, and realigns us with His purpose.

The Shepherd leads us along the familiar paths, shaping our steps in righteousness. Even when we don't feel His presence, His way remains imprinted in our hearts, reminding us of His love and truth. His guidance is not about control but about care, leading us to a life that honors His name.

†

FEBRUARY 7

He restores my soul; He leads me in the paths of righteousness for His name's sake. (Psalm 23:3)

Cultivate → The Shepherd doesn't just restore us—He redirects us. When we wander, He calls us back, not because we deserve it, but because His name and glory are at stake. His guidance is not about control but about care, leading us in righteousness so we can reflect His goodness.

Take a moment to reach out to someone who may feel lost or discouraged. Send a message of encouragement or share a verse that reminds them of God's restoring power. Just as the Shepherd pursues us, we can reflect His love by pointing others back to Him.

"Lord, thank You for restoring my soul when I stray. Help me trust Your leading and extend Your care to others who need to be reminded of Your love. Amen."

†

FEBRUARY 8

Yea, though I walk through the valley of the shadow of death, I will fear no evil; for You are with me; Your rod and Your staff, they comfort me. (Psalm 23:4)

Contemplate → How is it possible to walk instead of run in the *"valley of the shadow of death?"*

This valley represents the dark times in our lives—the distressing moments that box us in. Yet the Psalmist walks and *fears no evil* because the Shepherd is with him. He is with us, even when we feel surrounded by the *shadow of death*.

Ancient shepherds used the rod to protect their sheep from predators and the staff to rescue them when they wandered off. Likewise, the Lord protects and guides us, even when we can't see it, and we can find comfort in that.

†

FEBRUARY 9

Yea, though I walk through the valley of the shadow of death, I will fear no evil; for You are with me; Your rod and Your staff, they comfort me. (Psalm 23:4)

Cultivate → Walking through a valley can feel overwhelming, but the presence of the Shepherd changes everything. His rod defends, His staff directs, and His nearness dispels fear. You are never alone in the valley—the Shepherd is not behind you pushing, nor ahead of you waiting. *He is walking with you.*

Today, take a walk—whether indoors or outdoors—as a reminder of God's presence. As you walk, reflect on a past valley God has brought you through. With each step, recall how He sustained you, how He comforted you, or how He used that season to deepen your faith. Let this reminder give you confidence that the same Shepherd who guided you before will guide you again.

"Lord, thank You for walking with me through every valley. Help me remember Your faithfulness and trust Your leading in every season. Amen."

†

FEBRUARY 10

You prepare a table before me in the presence of my enemies; You anoint my head with oil; My cup runs over. (Psalm 23:5)

Contemplate → The Lord's table is a picture of His amazing grace. It is the place where we can release our fears, anxieties, and worries and receive His refreshing provision—even while surrounded by challenges and opposition. Notice that we are not removed from our enemies; rather, the Lord sets a table for us in their midst, displaying His peace and authority.

As God's guest of honor, He anoints our heads with oil, symbolizing His blessing and the power of the Holy Spirit in our lives. Just as a shepherd anoints sheep to protect them from pests and irritation, the Lord anoints us to guard our minds from the distractions and attacks of the enemy.

"My cup runs over" speaks of the abundance of His provision, not just enough to get by, but overflowing joy, peace, and favor. God does not merely sustain—He blesses beyond measure. At His table, there is always more than enough.

†

FEBRUARY 11

You prepare a table before me in the presence of my enemies; You anoint my head with oil; My cup runs over. (Psalm 23:5)

Cultivate → While the world often celebrates love in fleeting forms, the love of our Shepherd is unwavering and eternal. His love is so powerful that He sets a table of peace *in the presence* of our enemies—not after the battle, but right in the middle of it.

Take a moment to visualize this scene: You are seated at the Lord's table, your cup overflowing with His grace, your head anointed with His presence. *What enemies are you facing today?* Fear, doubt, opposition, unforgiveness? Release them to God, and rest in the truth that He has already made a place for you in His presence.

"Lord, thank You for preparing a table of peace for me, even in life's battles. Help me to rest in Your love and trust in Your overflowing grace. Amen."

†

FEBRUARY 12

Surely goodness and mercy shall follow me all the days of my life; And I will dwell in the house of the Lord forever. (Psalm 23:6)

Contemplate → The Hebrew word for *"follow"* here conveys the idea of relentless pursuit, much like an animal chasing its prey. However, in this case, it is not danger that chases us—it is God's goodness and mercy. His love is not passive; it actively seeks after us, covering the paths we walk and catching us whenever we stumble.

This promise is not temporary. The Lord's kindness and faithfulness pursue us all the days of our lives, from our first breath to our last. Even when life is uncertain, His mercy is unwavering.

The ultimate destination of the righteous is not just peace on earth, but an eternal dwelling in the house of the Lord. If His provision at the table is perfect, how much more perfect is His home? Psalm 23 is a journey from life's challenges under the Shepherd's care to the final promise of heaven in His presence.

†

FEBRUARY 13

Surely goodness and mercy shall follow me all the days of my life; And I will dwell in the house of the Lord forever. (Psalm 23:6)

Cultivate → As discovered yesterday, God's goodness and mercy don't merely follow at a distance—they pursue you relentlessly, like a Shepherd chasing after His beloved sheep. His love is not passive; it is active, seeking you out in every season of your life.

Instead of looking ahead in worry, take a moment today to look back in gratitude. Share your testimony of God's goodness with someone who may be feeling discouraged. Whether in a conversation, through a text message, or in a handwritten note, encourage someone with a reminder that God's goodness is still in pursuit—even when life feels hard.

"Lord, thank You for pursuing me with goodness and mercy. Help me to rest in the assurance that I will dwell with You forever. Amen."

†

FEBRUARY 14

Whoever walks blamelessly will be saved, but he who is perverse in his ways will suddenly fall.
(Proverbs 28:18)

Contemplate → The words *"perverse"* and *"preserve"* may look similar in spelling, but ironically, they represent complete opposites in God's eyes. This proverb highlights two distinct ways of life—two paths we can take, each leading to two very different outcomes.

Walking in integrity brings preservation, while choosing immorality leads to downfall. The verse doesn't promise a life without blame, but rather, that the one who walks blamelessly will be found righteous in God's sight. Integrity is not about perfection—it is about consistency.

And on a day when love is celebrated, we're reminded that the greatest expression of love is faithfulness—first to God, then to others. When we choose righteousness, even in unseen moments, we stand before the only Judge that matters, and His verdict is salvation. The choice is before us: will we be preserved in faithfulness, or will we fall through the deception of our own ways?

†

FEBRUARY 15

Whoever walks blamelessly will be saved, but he who is perverse in his ways will suddenly fall.
(Proverbs 28:18)

Cultivate → Integrity is the key to walking blamelessly before God. It's not about perfection but about consistency—choosing righteousness even when no one is watching.

Today, instead of focusing on what needs to change, take action by reinforcing what is already good. Identify one area where you have been walking in integrity, whether in your work, relationships, or personal discipline. Thank God for His strength in that area, and ask Him to continue preserving you as you walk blamelessly before Him.

"Lord, help me remain steadfast in integrity, not for appearance, but for Your glory. Strengthen me to walk blamelessly before You each day, that I may have the wisdom to do the next righteous thing for Your glory. Amen."

†

PART II

UNDERSTANDING

Proverbs & Psalms That Enlighten and Inspire:
The SUPPORT That Holds Your Mind & Guards
Your Heart!

FEBRUARY 16

He who is devoid of wisdom despises his neighbor, but a man of understanding holds his peace.
(Proverbs 11:12)

Contemplate → If peace can be held, it can also be dropped. A person of understanding does not just possess wisdom—they exercise it. Holding onto peace requires self-control, discernment, and love.

The contrast in this verse is sharp: those who lack wisdom quickly show contempt for others, but those who are wise hold back, knowing when to speak and when to stay silent. True understanding is measured in restraint, not reaction.

To be ruled by wisdom rather than impulse is to have a firm grip on one's thoughts and emotions. Holding onto peace means guarding it from being easily stolen by offense, anger, or pride. When we seek understanding, we gain the ability to navigate relationships with grace, responding in love rather than reacting in frustration.

†

FEBRUARY 17

He who is devoid of wisdom despises his neighbor, but a man of understanding holds his peace.
(Proverbs 11:12)

Cultivate → Yesterday, we learned that peace is a treasure, not something to be carelessly thrown away. A *man of understanding* knows that holding onto peace requires discernment, self-control, and love rooted in God's Word.

Today, put this wisdom into action. If you find yourself in a frustrating situation—whether a conversation, a conflict, or an internal struggle—pause before responding. Instead of reacting in frustration, take a deep breath and choose to hold your peace. Let your words and actions be guided by God's wisdom, not impulse.

"Lord, help me hold onto peace today. Give me discernment to know when to speak and when to stay silent, and let my heart be ruled by Your wisdom. Amen."

†

FEBRUARY 18

Teach me Your way, O Lord; I will walk in Your truth; Unite my heart to fear Your name.
(Psalm 86:11)

Contemplate → In this Psalm, David prays for understanding of God's way. When we say, *"Teach me,"* we must be open to His instruction, not just in theory but in action.

David immediately follows his request with a declaration of faith: *"I will walk in Your truth."* This is the heart of true discipleship—learning from God and committing to walk in obedience. By using the action of walking, David places the responsibility on God to lead his steps while affirming that he will follow.

He then prays, *"Unite my heart to fear Your name."* This is a request for focus and surrender. A divided heart is like a faulty compass—constantly spinning yet never pointing north. But when our hearts are united in reverence for God, we walk in unwavering faith. Understanding His way begins with seeking His will, surrendering to His guidance, and walking in His truth daily.

†

FEBRUARY 19

Teach me Your way, O Lord; I will walk in Your truth; Unite my heart to fear Your name.
(Psalm 86:11)

Cultivate → True learning begins with a heart willing to be taught. When we ask God to teach us His way, we invite Him to shape our thoughts, direct our steps, and align our hearts with His truth.

Today, instead of rushing through prayer, take a *prayer walk* as an intentional step of trust. As you walk, ask God to reveal a specific area where you need to align your life with His truth. With each step, silently pray, *"Lord, lead me in Your truth."* With each pause, ask, *"Unite my heart to fear Your name."*

"Lord, I open my heart to Your instruction. Teach me Your way, and give me the strength to walk in Your truth. Unite my heart to fear Your name. Amen."

†

FEBRUARY 20

The fear of the Lord is the beginning of knowledge, but fools despise wisdom and instruction. (Proverbs 1:7)

Contemplate → *"The fear of the Lord"* is the foundation of all true wisdom. It is not a fear that paralyzes but a reverence that awakens the soul. Without this reverence—this deep respect for God's authority—one remains spiritually blind.

This verse draws a stark contrast: those who embrace wisdom begin with fearing God, while fools reject wisdom altogether. To despise wisdom and instruction is to reject truth itself. A fool does not fail because of ignorance alone, but because of a hardened heart that refuses correction.

Everything begins and ends with God. If wisdom is our pursuit, then reverence for Him is our starting point. Without it, even the most intelligent mind is ultimately foolish.

†

FEBRUARY 21

The fear of the Lord is the beginning of knowledge, but fools despise wisdom and instruction. (Proverbs 1:7)

Cultivate → A heart that reveres God walks in wisdom. When we truly fear the Lord—not in terror, but in reverence—we align our priorities with His, allowing His wisdom to shape our decisions.

Take a moment to identify *one specific area* in your life where greater reverence for God would lead to wiser choices. Is it in how you speak? How you spend your time? How you handle challenges? Ask the Lord to help you walk in wisdom today.

"Lord, let my fear of You be the foundation of my decisions. Shape my heart to desire Your wisdom above my own. Amen."

†

FEBRUARY 22

Be angry, and do not sin. Meditate within your heart on your bed, and be still. (Psalm 4:4)

Contemplate → What is the answer to the distresses of the day? Lay down and *"be still."* It doesn't say, *"Do not be angry,"* but rather, *"Do not sin in your anger,"* which is often difficult to do.

Understanding tells us to retreat to our bed and *"meditate in our heart,"* then listen! *Meditate* means to reflect on God's promises, pulling out every substantial truth and claiming it as our own. In Hebrew, the word *"meditate"* is likened to what a cow does after grazing all day—chewing and re-chewing to extract every bit of nourishment.

After *extracting God's nutrients* within your heart, "being still" becomes active listening and waiting. You may not understand all that has happened in the day to bring you down, but knowing that God is in control is all the reassurance you need. Sometimes, we have to lie down in order to stand up stronger in faith!

†

FEBRUARY 23

Be angry, and do not sin. Meditate within your heart on your bed, and be still. (Psalm 4:4)

Cultivate → While this Psalm encourages meditation, it does *not* tell us to figure everything out. Instead, it points us toward the remedy for anxiety: *stillness in God's presence.* Overthinking strangles trust, but meditating on God's promises revives it.

Tonight, before bed, *pause and reflect* on God's faithfulness. Instead of replaying worries in your mind, turn them into a moment of worship. Choose one promise from Scripture and meditate on it as you fall asleep, allowing it to replace anxiety with trust.

"Lord, help me not to sin in my anger but to meditate on Your promises and find stillness in Your presence. Teach me to release anxiety and trust fully in Your control. Amen."

†

FEBRUARY 24

Go to the ant, you sluggard! Consider her ways and be wise. (Proverbs 6:6)

Contemplate → Understanding the ways of the ant brings clarity to this profound truth from Proverbs. The ant is diligent, efficient, and always preparing for what lies ahead.

This verse warns against laziness, which is not just about physical inactivity but spiritual complacency. A sluggard is held captive by distractions, mistaking idleness for rest. There is a time for rest and reflection, but there is also a time for action.

The ant works without constant oversight, yet it thrives because it follows its design. Likewise, when we model our work ethic after the ant, we live wisely—understanding that while God provides, He also calls us to sow in due season so that we may reap in the next.

Now is the time to wake up and be diligent!

†

FEBRUARY 25

It is better to trust in the Lord than to put your confidence in man. (Psalm 118:8)

Contemplate → This verse sits at the very heart of the Bible, serving as its central theme. In fact, Psalm 118 is not only at the center of the Bible in terms of chapters, but it also contains the very center verse of the entire Word of God: *Psalm 118:8*. This verse stands as a pivotal reminder to place our trust in God alone, rather than relying on human strength or wisdom. Consider these remarkable facts about Psalm 118:

1. The shortest chapter in the Bible is Psalm 117.
2. The longest chapter in the Bible is Psalm 119.
3. Psalm 118 is the center chapter of the Bible.
4. Psalm 118:8 is the central verse of the entire Bible.
5. There are 594 chapters before Psalm 118.
6. There are 594 chapters after Psalm 118.
7. This gives a total of 1,188 chapters, a symmetrical number that reinforces the significance of *Psalm 118:8*.

This verse is no coincidence—it reminds us that our confidence belongs in God, not man. Human wisdom is flawed, but God's truth is perfect and unchanging.

†

FEBRUARY 26

It is better to trust in the Lord than to put your confidence in man. (Psalm 118:8)

Cultivate → Consider the remarkable facts we referenced yesterday. Is this just coincidence, or is it a "Godincidence?" The central verse of the Bible reminds us that true security is found in trusting God. People, circumstances, and even our own strength will fail, but the Lord remains steadfast. When we build our confidence in Him, we stand on an unshakable foundation.

Today, take a step of faith by surrendering a specific worry or decision to God. Instead of relying on human advice or your own understanding, commit it fully to Him in prayer. Then, watch for how He provides guidance and peace.

"Lord, help me to trust You above all else. Teach me to place my confidence in Your unchanging character rather than the fleeting promises of man. Amen."

†

FEBRUARY 27

Go to the ant, you sluggard! Consider her ways and be wise. (Proverbs 6:6)

Cultivate → The ant does not delay or make excuses—it simply does what is needed in its season. Wisdom begins not with *knowing* what to do, but with *acting* on it.

What is one task you've been procrastinating that God may be calling you to address today? Whether it's a step of obedience, a conversation that needs to be had, or simply tackling something you've put off, commit to taking action before the day ends.

Even a small step forward is a step toward diligence.

"Lord, help me reject laziness and embrace diligence. Give me the wisdom to act today, rather than waiting for tomorrow. Amen."

†

FEBRUARY 28

I will remember the works of the Lord; surely I will remember Your wonders of old. (Psalm 77:11)

Contemplate → Memory is a powerful gift. What we choose to remember shapes how we respond to present challenges and how we trust for the future. This verse calls us to remember the works of the Lord—to deliberately recall the times He has moved, provided, and delivered.

The psalmist reminds us that our faith is strengthened not by forgetting our struggles, but by remembering God's victories. When doubt creeps in, looking back at God's past faithfulness assures us that He has never failed and never will.

Even our earthly fathers respond to our acknowledgment of "good gifts," so why wouldn't our heavenly Father? When we reflect on what He has done, we remind ourselves of who He is. His wonders of old are not just stories; they are proof that He is still at work. Do not forget to remember—because what He has done before, He can do again.

†

MARCH 1

I will remember the works of the Lord; surely I will remember Your wonders of old. (Psalm 77:11)

Cultivate → Intentional reflection strengthens our faith. When we actively recall God's past faithfulness, our confidence in His present and future provision grows. Remembering His wonders isn't about nostalgia—it's about trust that stands firm.

Take a moment to identify three specific ways God has worked in your life. How has He delivered you? Provided for you? Shown His presence in ways you couldn't deny? Whether big or small, write them down or meditate on them as a testimony to His faithfulness. Then, pray this or a similar prayer:

"Lord, I remember the wonders You have done in my life. Thank You for being faithful, even when I forget. Help me to trust in Your continued goodness as I walk forward in faith. Amen."

†

MARCH 2

The entrance of Your words gives light; it gives understanding to the simple. (Psalm 119:130)

Contemplate → You do not need to be book-smart, theologically brilliant, or worldly wise to understand God's Word. Just as a small candle, once lit, immediately illuminates a dark room, so too does the entrance of God's words enlighten any setting or mind that is settled and open.

"It gives understanding to the simple," not just the scholarly. It takes no degree of intelligence or exhaustive study of the Bible—just an open entrance for God's light to shine. His Word is not meant to be complicated or burdensome; it is meant to reveal truth, to make wise the simple, and to guide those who are willing to receive it.

God's Word *"gives understanding,"* it doesn't take understanding! If we make room for His truth, it will do the work of transforming us.

†

MARCH 3

The entrance of Your words gives light; it gives understanding to the simple. (Psalm 119:130)

Cultivate → Light exposes, reveals, and directs. The more we allow God's Word to enter our hearts, the more clarity we gain—not just about Him, but about ourselves.

Take a practical step today by reading a passage of Scripture with fresh eyes. Choose a Psalm, a Proverb, or a teaching of Jesus and ask, *"What is God revealing to me in this moment?"* Take note of one key truth that stands out and how it brings light to your current situation.

"Lord, open my heart to receive Your truth. Let Your Word illuminate my path and bring understanding to my mind. Amen."

†

MARCH 4

__Do not keep silent, O God! Do not hold Your peace, and do not be still, O God! (Psalm 83:1)__

Contemplate → Have you ever watched a chess master play? While their opponent may aggressively move pieces across the board, the chess master may sit quietly, unmoving—yet calculating. Each moment of stillness is intentional, part of a master plan that will unfold at just the right time.

Likewise, when God seems silent, it's not because He's inactive—it's because He's orchestrating His next move. In Psalm 83, the psalmist pleads for God to break the silence, but silence does not mean absence. Just as a chess master's stillness signals strategy, God's quiet seasons are often when He's working most profoundly.

When you feel like God is silent, trust that He's moving pieces you can't yet see. Keep praying, keep trusting, and wait for His perfect move.

†

MARCH 5

Do not keep silent, O God! Do not hold Your peace, and do not be still, O God! (Psalm 83:1)

Cultivate → Silence can feel like abandonment, yet God's stillness often signals strategy. Just as a chess master's quiet focus prepares for a winning move, God's unseen work is often positioning us for victory.

Today, instead of asking *"Why haven't You answered?"* ask, *"What are You preparing?"* In the meantime, write down one unanswered prayer you've been carrying and place it in your Bible. Let this act symbolize your trust that God is aligning His purposes—even when you can't see the moves He's making.

Keep that paper in place as a reminder that He is working in silence and that your story isn't finished yet.

"Lord, when answers seem delayed, teach me to trust Your timing. Help me to believe that Your silence is not absence but preparation for something greater. Amen."

†

MARCH 6

Pride goes before destruction, and a haughty spirit before a fall. (Proverbs 16:18)

Contemplate → Pride is deceptive—it blinds us to our own weaknesses while making us quick to notice flaws in others. It convinces us that we are always right, leading us further away from humility and wisdom. But destruction follows pride like a shadow—what begins as self-confidence can quickly become self-destruction.

Pride weakens our foundation, creating cracks beneath the surface that may not be immediately visible but are dangerous, nonetheless. It distorts our perception, making it easy to justify actions that should bring us to repentance. The remedy? Humility.

Understanding is recognizing when pride has crept in. Knowledge is applying God's Word to purge it. Wisdom is living out that humility before the fall ever comes. The question is—will we humble ourselves now, or will we wait for the fall to humble us?

Said differently—you can choose humility, or humiliation will choose you.

†

MARCH 7

Pride goes before destruction, and a haughty spirit before a fall. (Proverbs 16:18)

Cultivate → Pride is not just a personal struggle—it's a destructive force that can ripple into the lives of others. Left unchecked, it blinds us, isolates us, and ultimately leads to downfall. *On this day in 2009, my pride cost an innocent man his life.* What will yours cost you?

Pride convinces us that we are invincible, above correction, justified in our actions. But sin never stays contained—it spreads, wounding those around us in ways we often don't realize until it's too late. My choices did not just impact me; they shattered another life. And when the weight of what I had done finally settled, I had no escape, no excuse—only the reality of my own brokenness.

But here's the hope: God restores the humble. He lifts those who fall at His feet in repentance. The choice is ours—will we surrender now, or will we wait until the consequences force us to?

Today, take a step toward humility. Acknowledge where pride has taken root in your life. Is there someone you need to apologize to? A situation where you need to admit fault? Or maybe you need to surrender an area of pride to God before it leads to destruction. Do not let another day pass without taking action.

"Lord, break the pride that blinds me. Give me the courage to repent where I have caused harm and the humility to walk in Your truth. Restore what pride has broken and lead me in Your ways. Amen."

†

MARCH 8

Through wisdom a house is built, and by understanding it is established; by knowledge the rooms are filled with all precious and pleasant riches.
(Proverbs 24:3-4)

Contemplate → This Proverb isn't about constructing a physical house—it's about building a life. Your "house" represents your character, family, career, or ministry—whatever you are establishing. Wisdom lays the foundation, ensuring stability. Understanding strengthens and establishes it, keeping it firm through trials. Knowledge then fills the house, enriching it with God's truth, blessings, and purpose.

Without wisdom, the structure is weak. Without understanding, it won't last. Without knowledge, it remains empty. Every room represents what God entrusts to us—our relationships, responsibilities, and resources.

When we build according to His design, we create a home filled with lasting treasure, not temporary gain. If Christ is our cornerstone, everything we build will stand.

†

MARCH 9

Through wisdom a house is built, and by understanding it is established; by knowledge the rooms are filled with all precious and pleasant riches.
(Proverbs 24:3-4)

Cultivate → Every structure needs a blueprint, and every builder needs a plan. Whether you are constructing a family, career, ministry, or personal discipline, the foundation matters. Wisdom builds, understanding strengthens, and knowledge fills the house with lasting blessings.

Take a moment to reflect on what you are currently building in your life. Think about one specific area where you need God's wisdom, understanding, or knowledge to establish it firmly. Then, seek a Scripture that speaks to that area, and let it serve as the foundation for your next steps.

"Lord, help me to build my life on Your wisdom, establish my steps through understanding, and fill my days with the knowledge of Your truth. Amen."

†

MARCH 10

The secret of the Lord is with those who fear Him, and He will show them His covenant. (Psalm 25:14)

Contemplate → Do you tell secrets to those you cannot trust? Certainly not! Similarly, if God cannot trust us because we do not first trust Him, we will not be privy to the secret of the Lord. Remember from Proverbs 1:7, *"The fear of the Lord"* is the beginning of everything!

But often, it's through the *testing of our faith*—through trials, hardships, and the refining fire of life's struggles—that we come to know *His secret*. In those hard places, He reveals Himself in ways we could never learn in comfort. When we proclaim that God is King and His Son is our Savior, He invites us into a "whispered conversation"—the quiet assurance that comes when we submit to His authority and seek Him with reverence.

His secrets aren't hidden from us, but for us—reserved for those who truly seek Him. If we approach Him with humility and awe, He reveals deeper truths that transform our hearts and guide our steps. The deeper the trial, the clearer the whisper—for it's often in the heat of hardship that God reveals the heart of His covenant.

†

MARCH 11

The secret of the Lord is with those who fear Him, and He will show them His covenant. (Psalm 25:14)

Cultivate → God shares His wisdom with those who walk in reverence and trust. When we truly fear the Lord—not in terror, but in awe-filled submission—He reveals His covenant and guides us deeper into His truth.

Take a moment to evaluate your reverence for God. Are you living in a way that honors His covenant? Have you grown too casual in your walk with Him? Ask God to deepen your fear of Him—not to drive you away, but to draw you closer.

Choose one way to honor the Lord today. Spend focused time in prayer, confess an area of neglect, or study His Word with fresh eagerness. The more we seek Him in reverence, the more He entrusts us with His truth.

"Lord, I desire to walk in holy reverence before You. Show me Your covenant, teach me Your ways, and draw me closer to You. Amen."

†

MARCH 12

Give instruction to a wise man, and he will be still wiser; Teach a just man, and he will increase in learning. (Proverbs 9:9)

Contemplate → Instruction comes in many forms—advice, guidance, orders, and teaching. A wise person welcomes instruction, seeing it as an opportunity to grow and improve. To make progress in life, we must remain teachable.

My father once told me that being "teachable" is the mark of a great leader. How we respond to correction or rebuke reveals much about our character. While instruction can sometimes feel uncomfortable or even painful, those emotions are often what push us toward transformation.

Even a child can teach us valuable lessons, reminding us that wisdom isn't confined to age or experience. Stay open to instruction—whether it comes gently or sharply—and be grateful for every opportunity to grow. True wisdom is cultivated through humility, learning from both the expected and the unexpected.

†

MARCH 13

Give instruction to a wise man, and he will be still wiser; Teach a just man, and he will increase in learning. (Proverbs 9:9)

Cultivate → A teachable spirit is the mark of true wisdom. How we respond to instruction determines our growth. Correction can be uncomfortable, but those who embrace it gain greater understanding.

Think about the last time someone offered you advice or correction. How did you react? Were you open and receptive, or defensive and dismissive? God often teaches us through others, even in unexpected ways.

Today, choose humility by inviting instruction. Ask a mentor, friend, or family member for honest feedback in an area where you desire to grow. Rather than reacting, listen and reflect on how their words can sharpen you.

"Lord, help me to receive instruction with humility. Give me a heart that is eager to learn, knowing that wisdom comes from being teachable. Amen."

†

MARCH 14

Many times He delivered them; But they rebelled in their counsel, and were brought low for their iniquity.
(Psalm 106:43)

Contemplate → This Psalm highlights the Israelites' persistent pattern: despite God's repeated deliverance, they continually turned back to their own flawed counsel. Their rebellion ultimately led to their downfall, confirming Proverbs 16:18: *"Pride comes before destruction."*

Their story mirrors ours today. Ignoring God's guidance and relying on our own understanding often leads to failure and frustration. Yet embedded in their story is a powerful lesson: wisdom begins with learning from experience. A person is wise when they learn from their own mistakes—but far wiser when they learn from the mistakes of others. Be attentive to those God has surrounded you with—especially those who've passed through rough spots.

Keep your eyes and ears open for the *road signs* of what God is trying to show you. His warnings aren't roadblocks—they're detours designed to guide you safely forward.

†

MARCH 15

Many times He delivered them; But they rebelled in their counsel, and were brought low for their iniquity. (Psalm 106:43)

Cultivate → Rebellion always leads to downfall, but God's mercy offers restoration. The Israelites were delivered time and time again, yet they ignored God's wisdom and followed their own flawed counsel. Their pride led to destruction, and their disobedience brought them low.

Take a moment to reflect: Are there past mistakes or repeated struggles where God has been trying to teach you something? Sometimes we suffer because we refuse to learn. Instead of resisting His counsel, ask Him to reveal any areas where you need to surrender and grow.

Right now, think about one lesson you've learned the hard way. How has God used it to shape you? If there's still something you need to learn from it, pray for His wisdom to move forward.

"Lord, help me to learn from my mistakes and the experiences of others. Keep me from stubbornness and pride, and guide me in Your truth. Amen."

†

MARCH 16

For as he thinks in his heart, so is he. (Proverbs 23:7)

Contemplate → The mind is like the captain of a ship—where your thoughts steer, your life will follow. Imagine a ship drifting off course because the captain kept staring at the storm instead of the compass. The same happens when we fixate on fear, bitterness, or insecurity—our lives veer away from God's purpose.

But when we anchor our minds in God's truth, we stay on course. Thoughts of His promises keep us steady in uncertain waters, and a mind filled with His Word navigates us safely toward His will.

Your mind is the captain, and your thoughts are the wheel. Are you steering toward God's truth or being swept off course by negativity? Fix your mind on Him, and your life will follow in peace and purpose. And remember, the most powerful ship still requires course corrections to reach its destination—so train your mind daily to follow His direction.

†

MARCH 17

For as he thinks in his heart, so is he. (Proverbs 23:7)

Cultivate → Just like a ship's wheel must be adjusted to stay on course, your thoughts require daily correction. Each morning this week, pause and pray: *"Lord, align my thoughts with Your truth today."*

Then, throughout the day, whenever negative thoughts attempt to steer you off track, redirect your focus by recalling a specific promise from Scripture.

Additionally, encourage someone else to anchor their thoughts in truth. Send a message, write a note, or speak life into someone who may feel overwhelmed. As you help them recalibrate, you'll find your own mind more grounded in God's peace.

Finally, before you end your day, take a moment to reflect: *Where did my thoughts drift today? Did they point me closer to Christ or pull me away?* By practicing this, you'll become more aware of the direction your mind is steering.

"Father, train my mind to dwell on what is good and true. When fear or doubt try to steer me away, help me remember that You are my compass, guiding me back to Your perfect plan. Amen."

†

MARCH 18

Do not boast about tomorrow, for you do not know what a day may bring forth. (Proverbs 27:1)

Contemplate → When we spend time worrying about tomorrow, we miss the importance of today. God gives us what we need for each day, desiring that we focus on His daily provisions and purposes.

On March 6, 2009, I boasted about my tomorrow, and by March 7th, I had unintentionally taken a man's life while drinking and driving. You never know what a day may bring. My pride made me believe I was in control, but in a moment, everything changed.

Reflect on this: *Have you ever experienced a moment when pride or presumption clouded your judgment? How did God meet you in that moment?*

When we focus too much on tomorrow, we neglect the decisions we must make today. The support and wisdom God offers are only accessible in the present—don't miss their value by fixating on the future. Learn to value the importance and blessings of each day, for tomorrow will bring its own challenges.

†

MARCH 19

Do not boast about tomorrow, for you do not know what a day may bring forth. (Proverbs 27:1)

Cultivate → In Matthew 6:34, Jesus said each day has enough trouble of its own. Today is a gift—don't let worries about tomorrow steal its value. When we live for a future that is not promised, we neglect the moments that God has given us now.

Instead of worrying about what is ahead, be intentional about fully engaging in the present. Identify one way you can make the most of today—perhaps by reaching out to someone you've been meaning to encourage, spending meaningful time with a loved one, or finally addressing a task you've been delaying. Don't put it off until tomorrow—do it today!

"Lord, help me to embrace today with gratitude. Teach me to trust You with tomorrow and to walk in the purpose You have given me right now. Amen."

†

MARCH 20

Your word I have hidden in my heart, that I might not sin against You. (Psalm 119:11)

Contemplate → A heart filled with the Word of God is our first line of defense against sin. While we are sinners by nature, we do not have to live in sin. If you allow God's Word in, His Word will come out. Likewise, if you allow sin in, sin will come out.

What occupies your heart and mind will ultimately determine whether you sin or win. Sin doesn't only bring shame to us; it's an offense against our Creator and Savior, who shed His blood to purify us from our sinful ways. When God's Word is etched into our hearts through memorization, it will show up clearly in our character, conversation, and conduct.

Will you live in the victory that Christ already won? Let God's Word in your heart be the support that others can lean on in times of need. Remember, you may be the only Bible someone ever reads.

†

MARCH 21

Your word I have hidden in my heart, that I might not sin against You. (Psalm 119:11)

Cultivate → Most of us live with the luxury of having Bibles readily available—in our homes, offices, and even on our phones. Because of this, the urgency to store God's Word in our hearts may not seem as necessary. However, hiding Scripture in our hearts isn't just for times of persecution—it strengthens our faith, guards our steps, and prepares us for moments when we need God's truth immediately.

Commit to memorizing one verse (or this verse) today. Write it down, repeat it thoroughly, and reflect on how it applies to your life. Let it take root in your heart so that it strengthens you in temptation and equips you to walk in obedience to God.

"Lord, let Your Word be my guide and my guard. Help me to treasure it in my heart so that I may walk in Your ways and lead others to do the same. Amen."

†

MARCH 22

Turn away my eyes from looking at worthless things and revive me in Your way. (Psalm 119:37)

Contemplate → This Psalm serves as foundational support for the mind and heart and can be summed up in two words: *IGNORE MORE!* It's a request for God's help in turning away from worthless things that distract us from His excellence.

God's Word strengthens our vision, helping us see beyond the fog of distractions and keeping us on His path. The world constantly offers things that seem appealing but ultimately leave us empty. Even when we've given our attention to the worthless, the distractions, and wandered temporarily astray, it's never too late to ask, *"Revive me in Your way."*

Meditate on this Psalm and learn to ignore more, so that in doing so, you'll find the strength to stay pure and focused on what truly matters.

†

MARCH 23

Turn away my eyes from looking at worthless things and revive me in Your way. (Psalm 119:37)

Cultivate → *"Turn away my eyes."* Remember, distractions aren't just an inconvenience—they can rob us of the time and focus God has given us for His purposes. Social media, entertainment, busyness, and worldly ambitions often steal our attention without us realizing how much they've taken.

Today, take one practical step to limit distractions. Maybe it's setting aside a specific time to be phone-free, fasting from entertainment that pulls your heart away from God, or intentionally redirecting your thoughts when they drift toward the worthless. Identify one *worthless thing* that occupies too much of your time and replace it with something that revives your soul—prayer, Scripture, or worship.

"Lord, help me to turn my eyes away from what is fleeting and focus on what is eternal. Revive my heart in Your way, that I may walk with clarity and purpose. Amen."

†

MARCH 24

A fool has no delight in understanding but in expressing his own heart. (Proverbs 18:2)

Contemplate → The sign of a man who does not listen well is not forgetfulness or a short attention span. No! The sign of a man who doesn't listen well is one who only hears himself.

We learn best when we're willing to listen to more than just our own thoughts. A fool doesn't care about understanding the facts of life, but rather, he is consumed with his own selfish feelings. Instead of seeking understanding, a fool is already planning what he's going to say next—always topping others' stories with no lessons learned or gained.

But by embracing the truth in this Proverb, we can appreciate the flip side of the coin—the "head" of understanding, not the "tail" of foolishness. Take delight in listening well, and you will learn well, and all will be well. When you don't understand something, that's fine, but don't offer wordy evidence of that fact.

†

MARCH 25

A fool has no delight in understanding but in expressing his own heart. (Proverbs 18:2)

Cultivate → There's a difference between hearing and listening. True listening requires humility, patience, and a willingness to understand before responding. But fools, as this Proverb warns, only delight in expressing themselves rather than gaining insight from others.

Today, challenge yourself to practice *active listening*. Instead of waiting for your turn to speak, focus entirely on the person in front of you. Ask a thoughtful question before responding or simply reflect on what they've shared before adding your own words.

Learning to listen well is a mark of wisdom.

"Lord, teach me to be quick to listen and slow to speak. Help me seek understanding before offering my own opinions. Amen."

†

MARCH 26

Great is our Lord, and mighty in power; His understanding is infinite. (Psalm 147:5)

Contemplate → God is limitless! Even when life makes no earthly sense, we must remember that His understanding is beyond anything we could imagine. We often try to fit God into our human limitations, placing boundaries on what He can do. But why restrict an infinite God?

He cannot be measured, so why not allow Him to be the *Ruler* of your life? His power is unmatched, and His wisdom surpasses our own. When we stop relying on our limited understanding and fully trust in Him, our paths become clear. You don't have to carry the weight of figuring everything out—God already holds all the answers. If He has no wrinkle of worry, why should you?

His understanding upholds the heavens, while our own limited perspective often leaves us feeling burdened. Trust in the One whose wisdom is infinite.

†

MARCH 27

Great is our Lord, and mighty in power; His understanding is infinite. (Psalm 147:5)

Cultivate → Even on the days when we think we have it all figured out, we don't. Our perspective is limited, while God's understanding is infinite. He sees what we cannot, guiding us with perfect wisdom.

Today, humble yourself before His infinite knowledge. Acknowledge that He knows what's best, even when His plans seem unclear. Take intentional note of one area where you've been leaning on your own understanding instead of trusting Him. Surrender it in prayer:

"Lord, Your wisdom is beyond measure. Help me to trust Your understanding over my own, knowing that You see what I cannot and guide with perfect clarity. Amen."

†

MARCH 28

Counsel in the heart of man is like deep water, but a man of understanding will draw it out. (Proverbs 20:5)

Contemplate → Unless water is drawn from a well, it remains at the bottom, unused—good for nothing. The same is true for the emotions, wisdom, and experiences buried in the heart of a person. They remain untapped unless someone with understanding takes the time to draw them out.

A wise person does not settle for surface-level conversations but seeks depth, knowing that true counsel requires effort to retrieve. It is easy to keep what we know to ourselves or disregard what others may have to share, but a man of understanding thirsts for righteousness. He values wisdom, not just within himself but in others, knowing that drawing it out can lead to growth and strength for both parties.

Do not settle for shallow understanding—be someone who seeks and shares wisdom with intention.

†

MARCH 29

Counsel in the heart of man is like deep water, but a man of understanding will draw it out. (Proverbs 20:5)

Cultivate → Wisdom and emotion often run deep, but they won't surface unless someone takes the time to draw them out. People may hold back out of fear, uncertainty, or simply not knowing how to express what's inside.

Think of someone in your life who may need a listening ear. Be intentional in reaching out—ask thoughtful questions and create space for them to share. Whether through a conversation, a message, or a simple "How are you really doing?"—help draw out what is resting deep within. True wisdom and healing often begin with a willing listener.

"Lord, give me the wisdom to draw out counsel with understanding. Help me to listen well, speak with discernment, and be a source of encouragement to those in need. Amen."

†

MARCH 30

For the Lord gives wisdom; From His mouth comes knowledge and understanding. (Proverbs 2:6)

Contemplate → Got wisdom? Not unless it was given to you by God. Many seek wisdom from the world—through education, experience, or self-help philosophies—but none of it can truly enlighten life the way God's wisdom does. True wisdom is not achieved; it is received, given directly by the Lord.

Likewise, knowledge and understanding that are lasting and transformative do not come from human reasoning alone. You may gain knowledge from books and understanding from experience, but only what proceeds from the mouth of God will truly sustain and guide you. The question is, what are you leaning on? The world's wisdom or the Word's wisdom? One fades, the other remains.

Let His wisdom be the foundation that holds your heart and mind steady.

†

MARCH 31

For the Lord gives wisdom; From His mouth comes knowledge and understanding. (Proverbs 2:6)

Cultivate → Today is known as "April Fools' Day," a time when foolish fun is the norm. In contrast to this tradition, as believers, we are called to pursue wisdom, not folly. Even Christians can stumble into foolishness when we rely on our own wisdom instead of seeking the wisdom that comes from God.

Take time today to intentionally seek God's wisdom for a specific area of your life. Ask Him for the knowledge and understanding needed to navigate challenges, make decisions, or discern truth from deception. Then, take a moment to reflect: Are you leaning on your own understanding, or are you truly allowing God's wisdom to lead?

"Lord, I acknowledge that true wisdom comes only from You. Teach me to seek Your knowledge above my own, and keep me from the folly of trusting in worldly wisdom. Amen."

†

APRIL 1

***Your hands have made me and fashioned me; Give me understanding, that I may learn Your commandments.*
*(Psalm 119:73)***

Contemplate → Can a computer tell you what it was created for? No! It must be programmed and put to use by its creator. Likewise, we cannot define our purpose by simply looking inward or seeking answers from the world. True purpose is found only through the One who made us.

God's hands have not only shaped us physically, but He has also designed us with a specific purpose in mind. Yet, without understanding, we will struggle to live out that purpose. That's why the Psalmist prays, *"Give me understanding, that I may learn Your commandments."*

When we seek wisdom from the Creator and align our lives with His Word, we walk in the fullness of what we were made for. Understanding isn't just about knowing—it's about living out His commandments in daily life. I'd rather trust the Owner's manual—His Word—than attempt to configure my life on my own.

†

APRIL 2

Your hands have made me and fashioned me; Give me understanding, that I may learn Your commandments. (Psalm 119:73)

Cultivate → God's purpose for your life may not always align with your expectations, but His wisdom surpasses all human understanding. His hands have shaped you for a reason, and His commandments guide you toward that purpose.

Today, take a step toward discovering His plan by reading Psalm 139. As you read, highlight or write down any verses that stand out about God's design and purpose for your life. Let these truths remind you that you are intentionally created and called for His glory.

"Lord, You shaped me with a purpose beyond what I can see. Open my heart to understand Your ways, and help me walk in the purpose You have set before me. Amen."

†

APRIL 3

A fool vents all his feelings, but a wise man holds them back. (Proverbs 29:11)

Contemplate → Knowing when to express our feelings is important, but knowing *how* to express them is what separates wisdom from foolishness. Venting every emotion without restraint often leads to regret—words spoken in haste can wound others, stir up strife, and leave us feeling even more unsettled.

Just because we *feel* something doesn't mean we must *voice* it right then and there. Venting unchecked frustrations often fuels negativity rather than resolving it. While it's healthy to process emotions, wisdom teaches us to do so with patience and purpose.

Before venting, ask yourself: *Will this release bring peace, or will it prolong the tension?* A fool lets their emotions set them back, but a wise man knows when to hold them back—turning moments of frustration into opportunities for prayer, reflection, and growth.

†

APRIL 4

A fool vents all his feelings, but a wise man holds them back. (Proverbs 29:11)

Cultivate → Emotions are powerful, but wisdom teaches us how to steward them well. Not every thought needs to be spoken, and not every frustration needs to be aired. A wise person exercises self-control, choosing when to speak and when to be silent.

Today, take a practical step in mastering self-control over your words. Choose a verse about wisdom or patience (such as James 1:19 or Proverbs 15:1) and keep it in front of you—write it down, set it as your phone background, or place it somewhere visible. Before reacting to anything emotionally, read the verse and allow it to shape your response.

"Lord, give me the wisdom to know when to speak and when to hold back. Let my words be guided by Your truth, bringing life and encouragement rather than harm. Amen."

†

PART III

PRAISE

Proverbs & Psalms That Exalt The Christ:
The SUPPORT That Lifts Up the Spirit!

APRIL 5

My voice You shall hear in the morning, O Lord; In the morning I will direct it to You, and I will look up.
(Psalm 5:3)

Contemplate → Wake up sharp—in mind, body, and spirit—as the Psalmist declares, *"My voice You shall hear in the morning..."* As blessed as you are to open your eyes in the morning, send those blessings right back to God, who kept you while you slept.

Before you hit the ground running, begin with a smile. Studies show that smiling—even before your feet touch the floor—signals positivity to your brain and sets your mind in order. Afterward, let your first conversation be with God. As Psalm 5:3 declares, let your voice be heard in the morning as you look up in gratitude and trust.

Finally, take a moment to stretch—engage your body with purpose, thanking God for another day of life. When you start the day sharp in mind, body, and spirit, you position yourself to walk in step with Him. Remember: To keep from falling down through the day, you must first look up in praise!

†

APRIL 6

My voice You shall hear in the morning, O Lord; In the morning I will direct it to You, and I will look up.
(Psalm 5:3)

Cultivate → How you begin your morning sets the trajectory for your entire day. The first thing you focus on in the morning often shapes your thoughts and attitudes. Before checking your phone or jumping into your to-do list, take a moment to look up—literally and spiritually.

Start the morning with this simple routine:

1. **Smile** – Acknowledge the gift of a new day.
2. **Pray** – Direct your voice to God and thank Him for keeping you through the night.
3. **Stretch** – Feel the strength He has given you for another day.
4. **Look Up** – Set your focus on Him, trusting His guidance for what's ahead.

"Lord, before I do anything else, I turn my eyes to You. Let my first words of the day be words of gratitude and trust. Guide my steps and set my focus on You. Amen."

†

APRIL 7

Let another man praise you, and not your own mouth; a stranger, and not your own lips. (Proverbs 27:2)

Contemplate → Jesus never boasted about Himself, yet His life spoke volumes. If we are to boast, it should be in Him and what He has accomplished. Our words should be spent exalting Christ, not elevating ourselves. By doing all things for His glory, we align ourselves with the right side of praise—letting our actions speak louder than our words.

There's no need to broadcast your achievements or seek validation by drawing attention to yourself. God sees all things, and in His perfect timing, He will allow the right acknowledgment to come from others. True praise is best received when it's unsolicited and offered sincerely.

Instead of striving for self-promotion, focus on giving Christ all the props; and when we point the credit back to Him, He grants us access to His "Pops"—our Father in Heaven—who affirms and rewards us in ways far greater than human applause ever could.

†

APRIL 8

Let another man praise you, and not your own mouth; a stranger, and not your own lips. (Proverbs 27:2)

Cultivate → How often do you seek acknowledgment for your achievements? It is easy to desire recognition, especially when you've worked hard to achieve a goal. But true honor comes when we live for God's glory rather than man's applause.

Today, shift your focus away from seeking affirmation and toward serving with a humble heart. Look for ways to encourage or praise someone else instead. Whether through a kind word, a compliment, or a simple act of appreciation, take a moment to lift someone up without expecting anything in return.

"Lord, help me to live for Your glory, not for the approval of others. Let my actions speak louder than my words, and may my praise always be directed to You. Amen."

†

APRIL 9

From the rising of the sun to the going down the Lord's name is to be praised. (Psalm 113:3)

Contemplate → Just as the sun faithfully rises and sets, so should our praise flow continually. This verse is more than a call to worship—it's a reminder that praise is meant to cover every corner of our day and every area of our lives.

Geographically, the sun touches the earth from east to west—symbolizing the reach of God's glory. And spiritually, the Son's name is to be exalted from generation to generation. When you wake up in the morning, praise Him. As you walk through your day, praise Him. And when the sun sets, let His praise remain on your lips.

Even when circumstances feel dark, His light is never absent. So, no matter what season you're in, praise Him—because His presence surrounds you from sunrise to sunset.

†

APRIL 10

From the rising of the sun to the going down the Lord's name is to be praised. (Psalm 113:3)

Cultivate → This verse calls for continual praise, stretching across the globe and throughout the day. Praise isn't just for Sunday mornings or certain moments—it's meant to be woven into the fabric of our daily lives.

Today, set reminders at different points—morning, midday, and evening—to intentionally praise the Lord. Whether it's through a whispered prayer, a song, or thanking Him for something specific, make praise a rhythm of your day. Let it become as natural as the rising and setting of the sun.

"Lord, I want to praise You not just when I feel like it, but from morning to night. Help me develop a habit of continual gratitude and worship. Amen."

†

APRIL 11

The preparations of the heart belong to man, but the answer of the tongue is from the Lord. (Proverbs 16:1)

Contemplate → This verse is one of my favorite *ProPs,* and I've placed it in the **PRAISE** section because when we begin to prepare our hearts according to God's Word, praise naturally follows.

God controls everything—from the past to the present and beyond. Yet, He calls us to play an active role in preparing our hearts. When we commit to aligning our thoughts, desires, and intentions with His truth, He takes that preparation and directs our steps. The first step is ours—to prepare our hearts—and when we do, God steps in to guide our words, decisions, and outcomes.

Let us praise Him, knowing that even when we don't have all the answers, the *"answer of the tongue is from the Lord."* What flows from our mouths will reflect what has filled our hearts.

Preparation shapes the questions we ask, and by faith, we can trust that God is always the answer.

†

APRIL 12

The preparations of the heart belong to man, but the answer of the tongue is from the Lord. (Proverbs 16:1)

Cultivate → Are you preparing your heart daily to receive God's answers? The words we speak reflect the condition of our hearts. When we fill ourselves with truth, wisdom, and praise, our words will naturally reflect His goodness.

Choose one verse today to meditate on and store in your heart. Write it down, carry it with you, or speak it aloud throughout the day. When your heart is prepared with His Word, the answers that come from your lips will align with His wisdom.

"Lord, help me prepare my heart daily, so my words reflect Your truth and wisdom. Let the answers I speak be guided by You. Amen."

†

APRIL 13

He who sits in the heavens shall laugh; The Lord shall hold them in derision. (Psalm 2:4)

Contemplate → The Lord Jesus is coming again, and His triumph and kingdom within our hearts are our sacrifice of praise. This Psalm reveals God's response to those who attempt to oppose His divine plan—He laughs.

This isn't laughter of amusement but of sovereignty—a reminder that no rebellion can undermine His authority. Those who plot against Him will face the futility of their efforts. Yet, for those who trust in Christ, this truth brings comfort.

We can praise God that He "sits in the heavens," reigning with power and control. Even when the world feels chaotic, He is undeterred—fully aware of the outcome. Because Jesus is our Advocate and Redeemer, we can laugh with God, rejoicing in the security of His eternal plan.

Praise Him for His laughter, for it is better to laugh with God than to have Him laugh at you.

†

APRIL 14

He who sits in the heavens shall laugh; The Lord shall hold them in derision. (Psalm 2:4)

Cultivate → Imagine how our lives would look if we laughed instead of stressed when opposition came our way. God's Word tells us that it's possible—because that's what the Lord does! His sovereignty is unshaken, and so should our confidence be in Him.

Today, choose joy over anxiety. When faced with stress or opposition, take a moment to pause, breathe, and remind yourself that God reigns. Let your faith be stronger than your fear.

"Lord, thank You for being sovereign over all. Help me trust in Your plan, knowing that no human scheme can thwart Your purposes. May my confidence in You lead me to laugh with joy in the face of opposition, just as You reign above it all. Amen."

†

APRIL 15

The light of the eyes rejoices the heart, and a good report makes the bones healthy. (Proverbs 15:30)

Contemplate → Jesus said, *"The lamp of the body is the eye, and if your eye is good, your whole body is full of light"* (Matthew 6:22). How can you ensure that your eye is good and full of light, thus affecting the heart? By removing the shaded sunglasses of hypocrisy and looking to the "Light of the world, the *Son*."

The second part of this Proverb reminds us that our bones are healthy and strengthened by a "good report." A good report is more than just positive news—it's the truth that edifies and encourages. Whether you're receiving or giving a good report, praise should follow immediately.

By offering blessings to Christ through your words, your heart and your bones—your very being—will be nourished, bringing joy and prosperity.

†

APRIL 16

The light of the eyes rejoices the heart, and a good report makes the bones healthy. (Proverbs 15:30)

Cultivate → Be a source of good news today. Speak life and encouragement into someone's heart, and watch how their joy spreads to others. A kind word, an uplifting message, or simply sharing a testimony of God's goodness can make all the difference in someone's day.

Make it your goal to share a good report with at least one person today. Whether it's acknowledging their faithfulness, speaking hope into a situation, or sharing a verse that brings encouragement, let your words be filled with life. In doing so, you'll also feel the strength of God's light in your own heart.

"Lord, help me to be a vessel of encouragement. Let my words bring life, and may I be intentional about sharing the goodness of Your truth with others. Amen."

†

APRIL 17

Thus I will bless You while I live; I will lift up my hands in Your name. (Psalm 63:4)

Contemplate → Consider your hands. With them, we greet, eat, and touch gently. We write, turn the pages of the Bible, and lift up someone who has fallen. But with the same hands, we can punch, slap, or push down. We write hate, turn to pornography, and consume vices.

If I had to lift my hands in surrender and shame when I was arrested, how foolish would it be not to lift them in surrender to God's name? When we bless God with our mouths, we speak words of exaltation to His ears. But when we lift our hands, we show an act of dependence on the Father. This form of praise activates His heart.

If we pick up our children when they lift their hands to be carried, how much more will our Heavenly Father respond to our surrendered hands? He *props* up those who lift up their hands to His name.

†

APRIL 18

Thus I will bless You while I live; I will lift up my hands in Your name. (Psalm 63:4)

Cultivate → As you learned yesterday, raising your hands in worship is an outward expression of an inward surrender. It symbolizes dependence on God and trust in His provision.

Today, take a moment to physically lift your hands in prayer, whether in private devotion, during worship, or even in a quiet moment of surrender. Let this simple act remind you of your need for God's strength and His response to those who call on Him.

"Lord, I lift my hands to You in worship and surrender. Let my heart always be dependent on You, and may my praise rise as an offering of trust in Your name. Amen."

†

APRIL 19

***The king's heart is in the hand of the Lord, like the rivers of water; He turns it wherever He wishes.
(Proverbs 21:1)***

Contemplate → *"The king's heart"* refers to the heart of anyone in authority. While they may seem to control policies, decisions, and laws, the Lord is the true authority behind it all. Just as rivers of water may appear to flow randomly, God directs them as He pleases, and this He does perfectly.

There is purpose in every pattern of life. Rivers don't always follow a straight path—they twist, turn, and sometimes flood unpredictably. Yet God controls their flow to nourish the land. In the same way, He directs the hearts of leaders—even when decisions seem chaotic or uncertain—to accomplish His greater plan.

We should praise God, knowing that He controls every man's heart and every position of authority. Even when leaders make decisions that seem contrary to His ways, nothing is beyond His power. The Lord is the great Governor over it all. Ultimately, we must exalt Christ, from whom the channels of the heart are controlled and through whom the "rivers of living water" flow.

†

APRIL 20

The king's heart is in the hand of the Lord, like the rivers of water; He turns it wherever He wishes.
(Proverbs 21:1)

Cultivate → No authority exists outside of God's control. When circumstances feel uncertain, remember that He is the ultimate Ruler, guiding hearts and decisions according to His perfect will.

Take a moment today to pray for those in leadership—whether in government, your workplace, or even your home. Trust that God is at work, even when things seem out of control. Rest in the knowledge that His sovereignty reigns supreme.

"Lord, I trust in Your rule over all things. Turn the hearts of leaders toward wisdom and righteousness, and help me to trust in Your greater plan. Amen."

†

APRIL 21

For the Lord is great and greatly to be praised; He is to be feared above all gods. (Psalm 96:4)

Contemplate → You may say, "We don't have gods today," but anything we put before the one true God, the God of the Bible, becomes "a god." TV, money, status—anything that distracts us from our Creator can become a false god, sometimes even ourselves, with our own priorities and intentions.

"For the Lord is great," and if we truly understood what greatness means beyond the world's standards, we would praise Him greatly for His true greatness. Greatness is seen in His love, mercy, and power; it is the sacrifice of His only Son to save us. His greatness lifts us despite our sinful ways.

If we fully grasped the weight of Christ's sacrifice, praising Him above all else would be our natural response. Lift your voice and praise the One who is truly great!

†

APRIL 22

For the Lord is great and greatly to be praised; He is to be feared above all gods. (Psalm 96:4)

Cultivate → True praise is more than just words—it's reflected in our priorities and actions. One way to honor God's greatness is by actively replacing distractions with worship.

Today, take a step to put this into practice. Identify one distraction or habit that has been taking up too much of your attention, and intentionally replace that time with something that draws you closer to God. Whether it's spending extra time in prayer, reading Scripture, or listening to worship music, let your actions reflect your praise.

"Lord, You alone are worthy of my highest devotion. Help me to remove distractions and give You the praise You deserve in both my heart and my actions. Amen."

†

APRIL 23

By You I have been upheld from birth; You are He who took me out of my mother's womb. My praise shall be continually of You. (Psalm 71:6)

Contemplate → When my mother was pregnant with me, because of an illness, the doctor advised her to have an abortion. But what that doctor failed to understand was that it wasn't his decision to make, nor had the thought ever entered my mother's mind. She knew that though she carried me, it was God who *"upheld me from birth."*

For many of us, the attacks on our lives begin even before we are born, yet we serve a God who knew us before conception and is the One who brought us into the world. This verse is a powerful reminder that our very existence is by His design, upheld by His sustaining hand. No matter how chaotic life may seem, He has been there from the beginning and will continue to be. Our praise should be continually for God, for the protection and purpose He provided before we even took our first breath.

Have you praised God today for being the birth Specialist who knows best?

†

APRIL 24

By You I have been upheld from birth; You are He who took me out of my mother's womb. My praise shall be continually of You. (Psalm 71:6)

Cultivate → Your life is no accident. From the moment of conception, God has upheld you, sustained you, and guided your steps. A powerful way to acknowledge His hand in your life is by sharing your testimony.

Today, take a moment to reflect on a time when you clearly saw God's protection or provision. Whether it was a moment of deliverance, a season of healing, or a time when His presence carried you through, consider sharing it with someone—whether in conversation, in writing, or even on social media. Your story may be the encouragement someone else needs to hear today.

"Lord, thank You for upholding me from the very beginning. Help me to testify of Your faithfulness so that others may see Your hand at work in their own lives. Amen."

†

APRIL 25

In God (I will praise His word), In God I have put my trust; I will not fear. What can flesh do to me?
(Psalm 56:4)

Contemplate → In other words, *"In God (I will praise Jesus Christ)."* When we place our firm trust in God, we can be sure that no flesh can harm us or touch us unless God allows it. And even if we face persecution from man, we can rest assured that it is for our good when we love God and are committed to His purpose.

This Psalm of praise removes fear from our minds and replaces it with confidence in Christ. If God is for us, then no attack of man, no opposition, no hardship can separate us from His sovereign plan. Fear is a natural response to uncertainty, but trust in God is a supernatural response to His promises. When fear knocks, faith must answer. God is in control, and nothing—absolutely nothing—happens outside of His knowledge and permission.

If we trust in Him, we can confidently declare, *"What can flesh do to me?"*

†

APRIL 26

In God (I will praise His word), In God I have put my trust; I will not fear. What can flesh do to me? (Psalm 56:4)

Cultivate → Fear is a thief—it robs us of peace, joy, and confidence in God. But Scripture reminds us that fear has no place where faith abides. When we trust in the Lord, we no longer have to live captive to worry.

Today, take a tangible step to replace fear with faith. Write down one fear you've been holding onto. Now, find a promise from God's Word that speaks to that fear. If you're afraid of lack, cling to Philippians 4:19. If you're afraid of the future, hold onto Jeremiah 29:11. If you struggle with fear in general, meditate on 2 Timothy 1:7.

Once you have the promise, declare it aloud: *"In God I trust; I will not fear!"* Let His truth overpower your anxiety, and repeat this until faith replaces fear.

"Lord, You are my refuge and strength. I place my trust in You and refuse to let fear control me. Help me stand firm in Your promises and rest in Your peace. Amen."

†

APRIL 27

One thing I have desired of the Lord, that I will seek: that I may dwell in the house of the Lord all the days of my life, to behold the beauty of the Lord, and to inquire in His temple. (Psalm 27:4)

Contemplate → What is the *one thing* you desire of the Lord? This Psalm of David should be the constant hunger we seek to fulfill. Like Psalm 23, David again speaks of desiring to dwell in the *"house of the Lord"* all the days of his life. What life? Our earthly lives.

David understood that the closer we are to God's presence, the more His beauty rubs off on us. If our body is His temple and where Christ resides, then all the days of our earthly lives, we can bear *the beauty of the Lord* and find comfort in the "house" of His fellowship.

Make that *one thing* your only thing and praise the Lord through your persistence to be in His presence.

†

APRIL 28

One thing I have desired of the Lord, that I will seek: that I may dwell in the house of the Lord all the days of my life, to behold the beauty of the Lord, and to inquire in His temple. (Psalm 27:4)

Cultivate → Make dwelling in God's presence your highest priority. Life will always pull your attention in different directions but seeking Him first sets everything else in order. The more time you spend in His presence, the more you will behold His beauty, hear His wisdom, and be strengthened for whatever lies ahead.

Take a step today to prioritize God above all else. Before you dive into your tasks, worries, or distractions, spend time in His Word and in prayer. Let your "one thing" today be Him, and trust that everything else will fall into place.

"Lord, help me seek You above all else. Let my greatest desire be to dwell in Your presence, where true beauty and wisdom are found. Amen."

†

APRIL 29

Honor the Lord with your possessions, and with the first fruits of all your increase; So your barns will be filled with plenty, and your vats will overflow with new wine. (Proverbs 3:9-10)

Contemplate → This Proverb is not a formula for financial gain, as the world might perceive, but rather a call to honor and worship God with what He has entrusted to us. Giving our "first fruits" is an act of faith and gratitude, recognizing that everything we have—our time, talents, and treasures—already belongs to the Lord.

We are simply stewards of His provision. When we put Him first in our finances, efforts, and priorities, we position ourselves to receive His blessings in return. Even if you don't have a barn or a vat, when you offer the first and best of all He has given you, God's abundance will overflow into your life, both spiritually and practically.

Giving our first fruits says to God: *"I trust You enough to offer what I value most, believing You will provide all I need."* It is a cycle of trust, obedience, and blessing that glorifies Him and fulfills us.

†

APRIL 30

Honor the Lord with your possessions, and with the first fruits of all your increase; So your barns will be filled with plenty, and your vats will overflow with new wine. (Proverbs 3:9-10)

Cultivate → Are you honoring God with what He has entrusted to you? Your *first fruits* are not just financial—they include your time, energy, and gifts. It's easy to give God what's left over, but true worship is found in offering Him our best.

Choose one area in your life—whether finances, service, or personal time—and dedicate the first portion of it to the Lord this week. Be intentional about prioritizing Him first and trust that He will provide abundantly in ways beyond what you can imagine (Matthew 6:33).

"Lord, all I have comes from You. Help me to honor You with the first and best of what You've given me, knowing that Your blessings will always be more than enough. Amen."

†

MAY 1

He who finds a wife finds a good thing, and obtains favor from the Lord. (Proverbs 18:22)

Contemplate → After creating the world and declaring everything in it good, God said, *"It is not good for man to be alone"* (Genesis 2:18). Marriage is a divine institution, designed to provide companionship, support, and unity. If you have found a spouse of like mind, this Proverb assures you that you have found a *"good thing"*—but it doesn't stop there. It also states that in this union, you have obtained *"favor from the Lord."*

This is a sacred bond that lifts the spirit, strengthens the soul, and makes husband and wife *one flesh*. That's why I placed this in the *praise* section—because when you recognize your spouse as a gift from the Lord, your response should be gratitude.

Every *good thing* is a *God-thing*, worthy of praise.

†

MAY 2

He who finds a wife finds a good thing, and obtains favor from the Lord. (Proverbs 18:22)

Cultivate → Marriage is more than just companionship; it is a reflection of God's love and favor. A God-honoring marriage requires selflessness, commitment, and a heart that seeks to build up rather than tear down. Whether you're married or single, relationships in your life should reflect the love, patience, and grace of Christ.

Today, if you are married, take a moment to express gratitude for your spouse—whether through a kind word, an act of service, or a heartfelt prayer. If you are single, pray for God's wisdom and preparation, trusting that His timing and plan for your relationships are perfect.

"Lord, thank You for the gift of companionship. Whether in marriage or in friendship, help me to love others with Your grace and to honor You in all my relationships. Amen."

†

MAY 3

How sweet are Your words to my taste, sweeter than honey to my mouth. (Psalm 119:103)

Contemplate → Notice the physical comparison of honey in the mouth to the spiritual reflection of God's Word on the soul. This Psalm praises the excellence of eating, chewing, and consuming God's Word, making its satisfaction *"sweeter than honey."*

When we meditate on Scripture, we take in every nutrient, chew on it (breaking it down), swallow it (placing it in our hearts), and digest it (applying it to our daily walk). Meditating on God's Word is like savoring a rich meal—it requires time to sit with it, repeat it aloud, and reflect on its meaning.

God's Word will only taste good when consumed in this way. It is more than just words and stories—it is food that props up the broken spirit and drink that fills the heart and mind with the peace of God through Christ Jesus. Just as physical hunger leads us to seek food, spiritual hunger should lead us to God's truth.

Praise Him for giving us the taste buds for His Word and the ability to feast on its goodness daily!

†

MAY 4

How sweet are Your words to my taste, sweeter than honey to my mouth. (Psalm 119:103)

Cultivate → Just as a delicious meal takes time to savor, so does God's Word. When we rush through Scripture, we miss the richness of its meaning. But when we slow down and meditate on it, we allow it to nourish us deeply.

Today, choose one verse from the Bible that speaks to your heart. Memorize it, say it aloud, and reflect on its meaning. Let it settle in your soul like a sweet and satisfying meal. If possible, share the verse with someone else, offering them a taste of God's goodness.

"Lord, help me to savor Your Word, letting it fill and strengthen me each day. May its sweetness be the nourishment I seek above all else. Amen."

†

MAY 5

There are many plans in a man's heart, nevertheless the Lord's counsel—that will stand. (Proverbs 19:21)

Contemplate → This praise-worthy Proverb reminds us that no matter what we try to conjure up, it is the Lord's plan that will stand, and it always has our best interests at heart. Our hearts are filled with ideas, ambitions, and desires, but without God's direction, those plans can lead us astray.

It is much safer to stand on the Lord's counsel than to rely on our own limited understanding. The natural man gets caught up in his own reasoning, but the spiritual man submits to God's final word and guidance. While we may make plans that seem good in the moment, only God sees the full picture, and only His counsel is unshakable.

Praise Him for His wisdom and sovereignty, knowing that His plans are greater than our own.

†

MAY 6

There are many plans in a man's heart, nevertheless the Lord's counsel—that will stand. (Proverbs 19:21)

Cultivate → We often make plans with good intentions, but when our plans aren't surrendered to God, we risk striving in our own strength. Instead of forcing your own way, pause and ask, *Am I truly trusting God's counsel to guide me?*

Here's your challenge: Write down one plan, goal, or dream that's been weighing on you—whether it's big or small. Then, reflect on these two questions: *Have I genuinely invited God into this decision? Am I willing to let Him redirect me if needed?* Finally, place that plan before the Lord in prayer, releasing your grip and asking Him to align your desires with His greater purpose.

"Lord, I lay my plans at Your feet. Align my heart with Your will, and give me peace to trust that what You establish will endure. May Your counsel stand firm in my life. Amen."

†

MAY 7

O Lord, how great are Your works! Your thoughts are very deep. A senseless man does not know, nor does a fool understand this. (Psalm 92:5-6)

Contemplate → Our fragile minds cannot fully comprehend the thoughts of God. In Jeremiah 29:11, He declares, *"I know the thoughts that I have toward you, thoughts of peace and not of evil, to give you a future and a hope."* His plans for us are filled with purpose, far beyond our limited understanding.

Think of how humans struggle to understand even their own thoughts—how much more the infinite wisdom of God? His ways are higher, His works are great, and His knowledge is beyond measure. To deny the reality of His wisdom is to be utterly senseless. Even without sight, sound, taste, touch, or smell, the truth of God is written on our hearts.

Do not be foolish—praise Him for His magnificent works and His unfathomable ways!

†

MAY 8

O Lord, how great are Your works! Your thoughts are very deep. A senseless man does not know, nor does a fool understand this. (Psalm 92:5-6)

Cultivate → God's wisdom is beyond our understanding, yet His works surround us every day. Sometimes, we just need to slow down and notice. Today, take a moment to pause and praise. Instead of rushing through your routine, set aside a few minutes to simply acknowledge His presence. Whether it's in nature, in a conversation, or in an unexpected blessing, let your heart be filled with awe at the greatness of God.

Throughout the day, every time you witness something good, big or small, whisper a simple prayer of praise: *"Lord, how great are Your works!"*

This habit of gratitude will deepen your awareness of His presence and remind you that His hand is always at work in your life.

†

MAY 9

I will bless the Lord at all times; His praises shall continually be in my mouth. (Psalm 34:1)

Contemplate → Instead of always asking God to "bless me, Lord," this *ProPs of Praise* calls us to offer our blessings back to Him. Blessing the Lord at all times isn't just about words; it's about a lifestyle of gratitude and surrender. We bless Him when our character, conversation, and conduct reflect His goodness and grace.

Having *"His praise continually in our mouth"* means that our speech should be seasoned with grace, encouragement, and truth. It's easy to praise God when things are going well, but can we do it *at all times*—in the highs and lows, the triumphs and trials? True praise is unwavering, not dictated by circumstances but anchored in who God is.

Let this verse challenge you to develop a habit of continual praise, not just in worship settings but in the way you live every moment. Will you commit to a lifestyle of living this *at all times*?

†

MAY 10

I will bless the Lord at all times; His praises shall continually be in my mouth. (Psalm 34:1)

Cultivate → Praise should not be reserved for just the good times—it is a posture of the heart that remains constant in every season. When we praise God in difficulties, we declare our trust in His sovereignty. When we praise Him in joy, we acknowledge that all good things come from Him.

Today, be intentional about your praise. Set a reminder or create a habit of stopping at least three times throughout your day to lift up praise to the Lord. It could be a whispered *"Thank You, Lord,"* a short worship song, or even sharing a testimony with someone.

Let your mouth be a vessel of continual praise, no matter the circumstance.

†

MAY 11

For whom the Lord loves He corrects, just as a father the son in whom he delights. (Proverbs 3:12)

Contemplate → God's love motivates His correction. His discipline comes from a heart of deep affection, desiring lasting transformation for our good. Just as our earthly fathers corrected us—not out of anger, but to guide us onto the right path—God's correction is meant to perfect us.

When we face trials or receive His discipline, it's easy to resist or question His intentions. But discipline is not punishment—it is refinement. God's correction removes what is harmful and replaces it with what is holy. He does not correct us to shame us, but to shape us.

When we understand that His discipline is not to tear us down but to *prop us up,* we can praise Him even in the hardest moments of affliction. Yes, we can praise Him, for *His correction is for our protection.*

†

MAY 12

For whom the Lord loves He corrects, just as a father the son in whom he delights. (Proverbs 3:12)

Cultivate → God's discipline is a sign of His love, not His rejection. Instead of resisting His correction, embrace it as an opportunity for growth. Ask yourself: *Is there an area of my life where God has been refining me? Have I been ignoring His gentle correction?*

Take a moment today to surrender any resistance to His discipline. In prayer, thank Him for shaping you into the person He's called you to be. If there's a lesson He's been teaching you, write it down as a reminder that His love is at work in your life. Let His correction draw you closer to Him, knowing that He disciplines those He delights in.

"Lord, thank You for loving me enough to correct me. Help me to trust Your discipline and embrace the refining work You are doing in my life. Amen."

†

MAY 13

For You formed my inward parts; You covered me in my mother's womb. I will praise You, for I am fearfully and wonderfully made; Marvelous are Your works, and that my soul knows very well.
(Psalm 139:13-14)

Contemplate → You are one of a kind—*one of one*. We often see ourselves merely as products of our parents, but this *ProPs of Praise* reminds us that God personally and intentionally formed us. Every detail, every characteristic, every part of who you are was crafted by His hand.

It's easy to be discouraged by external factors—society's standards, personal insecurities, or comparisons—but God took delicate care in shaping your inward parts. His works are marvelous, and that includes you! You are fearfully and wonderfully made, *not by accident, but with purpose*. Instead of focusing on flaws, let your soul rejoice in the Creator's masterpiece—because that's exactly what you are.

Praise Him for His marvelous works, knowing that you are one of them.

†

MAY 14

***For You formed my inward parts; You covered me in my mother's womb. I will praise You, for I am fearfully and wonderfully made; Marvelous are Your works, and that my soul knows very well.
(Psalm 139:13-14)***

Cultivate → What do you see when you look in the mirror? Do you focus on imperfections or recognize the beauty of God's design? Let this verse challenge you to shift your perspective. You are not a mistake. You are a masterpiece.

Today, instead of being critical of yourself, take a moment to thank God for how He created you. Speak this verse aloud as a declaration of praise: *"Lord, I am fearfully and wonderfully made!"* Let this truth sink deep into your heart, reminding you that God's hands formed you with love and intention.

"Lord, I praise You for creating me with purpose. Help me to see myself through Your eyes and to celebrate the work of Your hands. Amen."

✝

MAY 15

For He shall give His angels charge over you, to keep you in all your ways. In their hands they shall bear you up, lest you dash your foot against a stone.
(Psalm 91:11-12)

Contemplate → Even Satan quoted this Psalm while tempting Jesus—so if the enemy knew its power, why don't we? This passage is a powerful reminder that God's divine protection surrounds us, and nothing can touch us without the Father's consent. Life may feel unpredictable, but this promise assures us that He has assigned angels to guard us in all our ways.

Sometimes, we may feel abandoned or unprotected, but even in the silence, God is watching, guiding, and sending help when we need it most. The hands of His angels serve as *props* to lift us up and shield us from destruction. This Psalm also prophetically exalts Christ, and because He has been lifted up, so shall our spirits be.

Even when the path is uncertain, we can rest in God's supernatural security.

†

MAY 16

For He shall give His angels charge over you, to keep you in all your ways. In their hands they shall bear you up, lest you dash your foot against a stone.
(Psalm 91:11-12)

Cultivate → God's care is both seen and unseen, working in ways we may never fully understand. This Psalm serves as a reminder to trust in His sovereignty rather than fear the unknown.

Today, take a moment to identify one area of your life where you need to *trust in His protection*. Is it your family? Your future? Your health? Pray over that area, thanking God for His angels and His covering. Then, consider committing Psalm 91 to memory, so when challenges arise, you have His promise already written on your heart.

"Lord, thank You for Your protection, even when I don't see it. Help me to walk in faith, trusting that You have placed Your angels around me. Keep me in all my ways and let my confidence rest in You alone. Amen."

†

MAY 17

__Praise the Lord! Praise God in His sanctuary; Praise Him in His mighty firmament! Praise Him for His mighty acts; Praise Him according to His excellent greatness! Let everything that has breath praise the Lord. Praise the Lord. (Psalm 150:1-2,6)__

Contemplate → Let ALL things praise the Lord! If you have breath, you have a reason to praise. When praises go up, the presence of the Lord comes down. God gives breath to every living creature, and every one of us should use that breath to glorify Him.

This is the power of praise—it lifts us beyond our problems and pain, pointing us to the peace and presence of His Name! The Psalmist ends with a resounding *"Hallelujah!"*—a call to worship, meaning *Praise the Lord!* When we lift up praise, we align ourselves with the truth of who God is, and we invite His presence to transform our perspective.

Praise is not confined to church walls it is the song of the soul, the breath of the redeemed. Praise Him in the morning, praise Him at night, and let His name be continually on your lips. *Hallelujah!* For He alone is worthy!

†

MAY 18

Praise the Lord! Praise God in His sanctuary; Praise Him in His mighty firmament! Praise Him for His mighty acts; Praise Him according to His excellent greatness! Let everything that has breath praise the Lord. Praise the Lord. (Psalm 150:1-2,6)

Cultivate → Praise is not just an *outward action*—it is an *inward posture* of the heart, acknowledging God's sovereignty and goodness. Through praise, we refocus our hearts on His greatness, shifting our attention from life's distractions to the joy found in Him.

Make praise a habit today! Set a reminder to pause three times—morning, midday, and evening—to say, *"Praise the Lord!"* aloud. Let this simple act redirect your focus and remind you of His excellent greatness.

"Lord, I lift my praise to You today! May my heart and mouth always declare Your goodness, and may Your name be continually on my lips. Amen."

†

Matthew Maher

PART IV
PERSERVERANCE

Proverbs & Psalms That Enhance One's Faith:
The SUPPORT That Presses You Forward Against
The Wind!

MAY 19

For the Lord will be your confidence, and will keep your foot from being caught. (Proverbs 3:26)

Contemplate → The Lord's confidence is like an anchor in stormy seas. When the winds howl, the waves crash, and everything feels chaotic, His presence holds you steady. Even when circumstances try to knock you off course, God keeps your footing secure under His guidance.

The Christian walk is not easy, but boldness in Christ enables you to endure, no matter the pressure or the snares that seek to entangle you. Like a climber scaling a rocky path, your grip must remain firm on the Rock of Christ. The enemy will try to shake your foundation, but God is your steady ground.

Place your trust in the Lord, and He will be the confidence that strengthens your faith, carrying you forward—even beyond your own ability. His support is all we need to stand firm and press on.

†

MAY 20

For the Lord will be your confidence, and will keep your foot from being caught. (Proverbs 3:26)

Cultivate → Confidence in the Lord is not self-reliance—it is faith in His power to hold you steady. Instead of relying on your own strength, surrender your uncertainties to Him and walk boldly in His assurance.

Take a physical step of faith today. Whether it's initiating a conversation, making a difficult decision, or stepping outside your comfort zone, do it with the confidence that *God goes before you*. As you take that step, declare: *"The Lord is my confidence; He secures my steps!"*

"Lord, I release my doubts and fears to You. Help me walk in confidence, knowing that You hold my steps firm. Amen."

†

MAY 21

Blessed are those who keep justice, and he who does righteousness at all times. (Psalm 106:3)

Contemplate → Integrity is like a compass—pointing you to what is right, even when pressure tries to pull you off course. Just as a hiker trusts his compass to guide him safely through the wilderness, we must trust God's moral compass to guide us through life's challenges.

"I will not compromise" is not just a decision—it's a lifestyle that never rests. It embodies a *righteousness at all times* mindset. The truest definition of integrity is "doing what is right, no matter who is watching."

This Psalm proclaims a state of happiness ("blessed") for those who keep justice, which means choosing to do what is right even when it's unpopular or inconvenient. Integrity isn't a sometimes thing—it's an always thing.

When you commit to living without compromise, no matter the obstacles you face, you are embracing perseverance—pressing through (*per*) the most difficult circumstances (*severe*). Keep justice, and God will keep you!

†

MAY 22

Blessed are those who keep justice, and he who does righteousness at all times. (Psalm 106:3)

Cultivate → Integrity is built through consistent choices, not just big moments. Every small decision to do what's right shapes your character and strengthens your faith.

Today, identify one situation where you can intentionally choose integrity over convenience. It could be in your workplace, your home, a conversation, or even a private thought. Make the choice to do what is right, even if no one sees—but God does.

"Lord, help me walk in righteousness at all times. Strengthen my heart to choose what is right, no matter the cost. Amen."

†

MAY 23

If you faint in the day of adversity, your strength is small. (Proverbs 24:10)

Contemplate → Trouble doesn't create weakness; it exposes it. Trials and hardships are like a weightlifter testing their limits—revealing the strength they have been building beneath the surface.

Adversity doesn't weaken faith—it reveals where your faith stands and where it needs strengthening. If you faint in the day of adversity, it's not because the battle is too great—it's because your strength is too small.

But here's the hope: your strength doesn't have to stay small. A person whose heart is rooted in Christ can face any trial, just as David stood before Goliath, knowing that God fights for him. *"For His strength is made perfect in our weakness"* (2 Corinthians 12:9).

Courage isn't the absence of fear—it's the refusal to let fear dictate your response. Let this Proverb of Perseverance remind you that the greater the battle, the greater the opportunity to show that Christ is your strength. Stand firm and watch your Goliath fall.

†

MAY 24

If you faint in the day of adversity, your strength is small. (Proverbs 24:10)

Cultivate → Adversity doesn't weaken faith—it reveals it. It shows what's truly within us and where we need God's strength to sustain us.

Instead of feeling defeated by hardship, invite God into the battle. Take a moment today to *pray for perseverance* in a specific challenge you're facing. Ask God to increase your faith and give you the strength to stand firm.

"Lord, when adversity comes, let my faith be strong. Strengthen my heart so that I do not faint, but trust in Your power to carry me through. I stand in Your strength today. Amen."

†

MAY 25

When you said, "Seek My face," my heart said to You, "Your face Lord, I will seek." (Psalm 27:8)

Contemplate → God is always inviting us to seek Him, but are we responding with urgency, or allowing the noise of life to drown Him out? David's answer was immediate and from the heart—he didn't hesitate or make excuses. When our hearts are truly in tune with God, our response will mirror David's: *"Your face, Lord, I will seek."*

Distractions and demands will always compete for our attention, pulling us away from spending time with the Lord. But seeking Him is the key to strengthening our faith and standing firm in a chaotic world.

To seek His face is to pursue His presence, to hunger for a deeper relationship, and to align our hearts with His will.

As you listen in stillness, ask God to reveal one area where He's calling you to deeper trust. Sometimes, we must silence our own thoughts and the voices of the world to hear His whisper: *"Seek My face."* Let your heart answer, and in doing so, you'll find the peace, strength, and perseverance you need.

†

MAY 26

When you said, "Seek My face," my heart said to You, "Your face Lord, I will seek." (Psalm 27:8)

Cultivate → God's voice isn't found in the chaos—it's heard in quiet surrender. Seeking His face requires intentional time, free from distractions, where we can tune our hearts to hear Him.

Today, set aside time to be still before the Lord. Find a quiet space, turn off distractions, and sit in His presence. Rather than speaking first, *listen*—let His Spirit guide your thoughts. As you seek Him, ask: *"Lord, what do You want me to know today?"*

"Father, I choose to seek Your face above all else. Quiet my heart and open my ears to hear Your voice. Help me desire Your presence more than the distractions of this world. Amen."

†

MAY 27

The lazy man will not plow because of winter; He will beg during harvest and have nothing. (Proverbs 20:4)

Contemplate → Keep plowing. Keep planting. Keep sowing. In due season, you will reap what you have sown. The *lazy man* refuses to work because of unfavorable conditions, failing to recognize that every harvest begins with faithfulness in the hard seasons. If you don't plow when it's difficult, you won't reap when it's time.

Too often, we allow cold circumstances, hardships, or discouragement to stop us from pressing forward in faith. But spiritual perseverance means working even when the conditions aren't ideal. The farmer doesn't wait for perfect weather to plant—he knows that the harvest depends on what he sows today.

Do not let spiritual laziness rob you of the blessings God intends for you. *Plow the field* He has given you, and trust that *He will bring the increase* in His perfect time.

†

MAY 28

The lazy man will not plow because of winter; He will beg during harvest and have nothing. (Proverbs 20:4)

Cultivate → What "fields" in your life need plowing despite tough circumstances? Maybe it's your faith, relationships, work, or calling—whatever it is, don't delay just because conditions seem difficult.

Today, commit to sowing effort where it's needed. Identify an area where you've hesitated due to discomfort or hardship. Take one practical step forward—whether it's making a decision, starting a task, or stepping out in faith. Trust God for the harvest, knowing He blesses diligence.

"Lord, help me to persevere through challenges, trusting that You are working even when I don't see the results yet. Give me the strength to keep plowing and the faith to trust You with the harvest. Amen."

†

MAY 29

You will show me the path of life; In Your presence is fullness of joy; At your right hand are pleasures forevermore. (Psalm 16:11)

Contemplate → Picture God's path as a lantern-lit trail in the forest—each step reveals just enough light to take the next step with confidence. While the journey may feel uncertain, His presence leads you one step at a time.

Jesus endured suffering *"for the joy set before Him"* and we are called to do the same (Hebrews 12:2). True *fullness of joy* is found in the presence of God, not in fleeting worldly pleasures. Victory is already secured through Christ, and by walking His path, we find purpose, perseverance, and promise.

Let this *Psalm of Perseverance* strengthen your heart. You are not wandering—God is leading. Follow His path with confidence, knowing that He is both the destination and the way.

†

MAY 30

You will show me the path of life; In Your presence is fullness of joy; At your right hand are pleasures forevermore. (Psalm 16:11)

Cultivate → God's path leads to lasting joy, not temporary happiness. Consider what *"fullness of joy"* means to you. Have you truly experienced it in His presence?

Instead of chasing after momentary fulfillment, commit to staying on God's path, where eternal joy is found. Today, take time to be in His presence—whether through worship, prayer, or meditating on His Word—and allow Him to fill you with His joy.

"Lord, keep my feet on the path of life. Let me not seek fulfillment in anything apart from You, for only in Your presence is true joy. Amen."

†

MAY 31

My son, do not forget my law, but let your heart keep my commands; For length of days and long life and peace they shall add to you. (Proverbs 3:1-2)

Contemplate → Consider how the words *"law"* and *"commands"* can feel restrictive, but in God's hands, they are meant to bring freedom and fullness of life. This Proverb reveals a *cause-and-effect principle*—when we hold fast to God's law and treasure His commands in our hearts, we gain *length of days, a long life, and peace.*

The key to keeping God's commands is *love*—love for Him and love for others. His Word lifts us up, while the ways of the world pull us down. When we align our hearts with God's law, we experience the peace that only He can give.

God's commands are not burdens to carry; they are boundaries of blessing. Hold on to them, let them shape your heart, and watch how they add life and peace to your days.

†

JUNE 1

My son, do not forget my law, but let your heart keep my commands; For length of days and long life and peace they shall add to you. (Proverbs 3:1-2)

Cultivate → God's commands are not just meant to be read but *lived out.* Choose one command today to intentionally put into practice—whether it's loving your neighbor, forgiving someone, or speaking truth with grace. As you keep His command, take note of how it affects your heart, your relationships, and your peace.

By the end of the day, share your experience with one person. Let your obedience be a testimony of the life and peace that come from walking in God's ways.

"Lord, help me not just hear Your commands but live them out. Let my obedience bring peace and life, drawing me closer to You. Amen."

†

JUNE 2

Be still and know that I am God; I will be exalted among the nations, I will be exalted in the earth.
(Psalm 46:10)

Contemplate → This Psalm calls us to a *posture of stillness*, not passivity. In a world that moves at high speed, where chaos often dictates our emotions, God's command is simple: *Stop. Be still. Know.* When everything around us is rushing and restless, our natural tendency is to move with it, react to it, or even try to control it. But here, God reminds us that true strength is found in *stillness*—not stillness for its own sake, but a stillness rooted in knowing who He is.

A stilled heart is like a calm lake that reflects the sky above—when our hearts are quiet, we become better mirrors of God's peace. Just as ripples disturb the reflection on the water, so does worry disrupt our trust in Him. When we stop striving and simply trust in who He is, we allow His power and presence to take over. He alone is exalted, not just in the grand scheme of the nations, but in the smallest details of our lives.

Maybe today, God is calling you to pause, to notice, to trust. His voice is clearest in the stillness.

†

JUNE 3

Be still and know that I am God; I will be exalted among the nations, I will be exalted in the earth. (Psalm 46:10)

Cultivate → Stillness is an intentional act of trust—one that requires patience and surrender. Set aside five minutes today to sit in complete silence before God. No distractions, no requests—just stillness. As you do, focus on this truth: *God is in control.*

Resist the urge to fill the silence with words or thoughts. Instead, embrace the quiet and allow your heart to settle in His presence. Breathe deeply, reflect on His faithfulness, and rest in the assurance that He reigns over every detail of your life.

When your time of stillness ends, don't rush back into the noise. Carry that posture of peace with you throughout the day, allowing His stillness to calm your mind and steady your heart. Remember, He is exalted over all things—both seen and unseen.

"Lord, help me to quiet my heart before You. In stillness, let me know You more, trust You deeper, and find peace in Your perfect control. Amen."

†

JUNE 4

He who walks with integrity, walks securely, but he who perverts his ways will become known.
(Proverbs 10:9)

Contemplate → There are two ways to walk, and each will face trials and tough decisions—but only one brings *security*. The path of *integrity* may not always be the easiest, but it is the only one that stands firm. Like a well-built foundation, integrity holds steady under pressure, while the crooked path crumbles under scrutiny.

Notice that *"he who perverts his ways will become known."* This means deception and dishonesty will eventually be exposed. Those who take shortcuts or compromise their character may seem to advance for a time, but the truth always surfaces. Walking with integrity means choosing to do what is right even when no one is watching—because in reality, *God always is.*

The straight path may be narrow, but it is the one that leads to true security.

†

JUNE 5

He who walks with integrity, walks securely, but he who perverts his ways will become known.
(Proverbs 10:9)

Cultivate → Integrity is built through daily choices, and each decision we make strengthens the foundation of our character. Today, commit to one intentional act of integrity—whether it's being honest in a tough situation, standing firm in your convictions, or choosing *righteousness over convenience*. Integrity isn't just about the big moments; it's about the unseen, everyday decisions that define who you are.

Even the smallest choice can reinforce the security of your walk. Ask God to guide your steps and reveal any areas where your integrity needs to grow. Then, trust that as you walk in truth, His peace will surround you.

"Lord, keep my steps aligned with Your truth. Strengthen me to walk with integrity, even when no one else sees. Let my life reflect Your righteousness in every decision I make. Amen."

†

JUNE 6

So teach us to number our days that we may gain a heart of wisdom. (Psalm 90:12)

Contemplate → This Psalm, written by Moses, is a powerful reminder of life's brevity and the value of perseverance. He prayed, *"Teach us to number our days,"* not so we would fear time slipping away, but so we would use it wisely. Each day is an opportunity to live with purpose, pursue righteousness, and invest in what matters eternally.

When we embrace the temporary nature of life and commit to suffering well, we begin to *gain a heart of wisdom*. Wisdom isn't just about knowing what to do—it's about knowing why it matters. Every moment spent in obedience to God is a building block for eternity.

Instead of letting time pass without intention, let each day prop you up toward greater wisdom, deeper faith, and a life well-lived in His presence.

†

JUNE 7

So teach us to number our days that we may gain a heart of wisdom. (Psalm 90:12)

Cultivate → Your time is one of the most valuable resources God has given you. How are you investing it? Take a moment to reflect on your daily routines—are they drawing you closer to God or just keeping you busy?

This week, make one small change to prioritize eternal pursuits—whether it's spending more time in prayer, reducing distractions, or focusing on serving others. If it works well, challenge yourself to add another adjustment next week, and continue building a life of wisdom and purpose.

"Lord, help me to number my days with intention. Teach me to use my time wisely and to seek eternal things above temporary distractions. Amen."

†

JUNE 8

As a dog returns to his own vomit, so a fool repeats his folly. (Proverbs 26:11)

Contemplate → Mistakes are unavoidable, but what matters most is how we respond to them. Do we learn, grow, and press forward? Or do we, like a dog, return to the very thing that made us sick?

A *"fool repeats his folly,"* choosing comfort over change and pride over progress. But a wise man learns from his past, refusing to return to what once enslaved him. This Proverb serves as both a warning and encouragement—warning us against habitual sin but encouraging us to break the cycle and move forward.

God has not called you back to your filth but forward into freedom.

†

JUNE 9

As a dog returns to his own vomit, so a fool repeats his folly. (Proverbs 26:11)

Cultivate → Breaking free from repeated folly starts with recognition and a decision to move forward in God's strength. Identify one area in your life where you keep returning to the same mistake. Be honest, then surrender it fully to the Lord.

Instead of relying on willpower alone, surround yourself with accountability, truth, and God's wisdom to help you resist the cycle. Memorize a Scripture that speaks to this struggle and use it as a weapon when temptation arises.

"Lord, help me to learn from my mistakes and not return to the things that hinder my growth in You. Give me wisdom to overcome, strength to press forward, and discernment to avoid the traps of repeated folly. Amen."

†

JUNE 10

***Wait on the Lord; Be of good courage, and He shall strengthen your heart; Wait, I say, on the Lord.
(Psalm 27:14)***

Contemplate → God's timing is never early and never late—it is perfect. Even when waiting feels like a struggle, remember that *waiting on the Lord* is an act of trust, not inactivity.

You may feel restless, but courage is built in the waiting. Your faith is strengthened when you choose to trust instead of rush. Anxiety tells us to force our way forward, but God's Word reminds us to *stand firm and wait.* When we wait in expectation, not frustration, our hearts become anchored in His promises.

So, take a deep breath, and rest in His perfect timing. *"Wait, I say, on the Lord!"*

†

JUNE 11

***Wait on the Lord; Be of good courage, and He shall strengthen your heart; Wait, I say, on the Lord.
(Psalm 27:14)***

Cultivate → When waiting feels hard, truth must be louder than doubt. Impatience can make us restless, but anchoring ourselves in God's Word renews our strength. Commit this verse to memory so that when discouragement whispers, you have His promise ready to declare over your heart.

Try this practical step: Write Psalm 27:14 down three times, read it aloud each time, and then send it to a friend who may also need encouragement. Repetition helps to seal Scripture in your heart, and sharing it strengthens others as well. By internalizing His Word, you'll find it easier to cling to His peace when waiting feels overwhelming.

"Lord, help me to trust in Your perfect timing. Strengthen my heart as I wait on You, and give me the courage to rest in Your plan instead of my own. Remind me that Your timing is never late and always best. Amen."

†

JUNE 12

Keep your heart with all diligence for out of it springs the issues of life. (Proverbs 4:23)

Contemplate → Guarding your heart is a daily discipline, not an occasional practice. The core of your being—your heart—directs every word, action, and thought. If your heart is left unguarded, life's distractions, temptations, and pressures will pull you in every direction.

In a world full of noise and chaos, keeping your heart steady and rooted in Christ is the only way to remain *diligent and unshaken.* Guarding your heart isn't about building walls of isolation; it's about establishing boundaries that protect what God is cultivating within you.

When adversity comes, will you react in frustration or respond in faith? The standard you set for guarding your heart is the standard that will shape your life. What you allow into your heart—whether through what you watch, listen to, or dwell on—will ultimately influence what flows out.

Keep it strong, keep it pure, and above all, keep it focused on the Lord.

†

JUNE 13

Keep your heart with all diligence for out of it springs the issues of life. (Proverbs 4:23)

Cultivate → What you allow into your heart will shape what flows out of your life. Just as a well must be protected from contamination, your heart must be guarded against negativity, distractions, and sin.

Today, take one step to better guard your heart. Maybe it's limiting social media, filtering the conversations you engage in, or filling your mind with God's Word instead of the world's noise. Choose one intentional way to protect your heart and keep it set on Christ.

"Lord, help me guard my heart with diligence. Let my thoughts, words, and actions reflect Your truth and not the distractions of this world. Amen."

†

JUNE 14

For this is God, our God forever and ever; He will be our guide even to death. (Psalm 48:14)

Contemplate → We serve a God who leads us through everything, even to death itself. He is not a distant deity watching from afar but an *ever-present guide* who has already conquered every path we will walk.

When life's trials seem overwhelming—even to destruction, even to disease, even to death—we must remember that *He is still God, our God, forever and ever*. No circumstance is beyond His reach. However, we must actively engage our faith in His guidance, trusting that every experience is shaping and strengthening us.

Do not let fear or doubt drag your eyes downward in defeat. Instead, look up to the One who is guiding you. For those in Christ, even to death is life.

†

JUNE 15

For this is God, our God forever and ever; He will be our guide even to death. (Psalm 48:14)

Cultivate → God has never failed you, and He never will. Think back to a time when He guided you through uncertainty. What were you worried about? How did He bring resolution? Reflect on His faithfulness in the past as a reminder that He is guiding you now and will continue to do so forever.

Take a few moments to thank God for His leadership in your life. Then, share a testimony with someone about how He has been your guide. Your faith journey may encourage someone else to trust Him more.

"Lord, thank You for leading me every step of the way. Even when I cannot see the path ahead, I trust in Your guidance. You are my God forever and ever. Amen."

†

JUNE 16

When a man's ways please the Lord, He makes even his enemies to be at peace with him. (Proverbs 16:7)

Contemplate → Living a life that pleases the Lord does not mean living without opposition. In fact, when we walk in integrity and righteousness, we often face resistance from the world. However, this Proverb reminds us that God is the one who brings peace, *even with our enemies.*

Faith is developed through struggle, but when our focus is on pleasing God rather than fighting for our own reputation, He props us up above contention. Our efforts to please the Lord are always worth the attacks we may endure. Instead of wasting energy battling our accusers, we are called to trust in the Lord to be our answer and our victory.

Perseverance brings peace—not by avoiding conflict, but by aligning our ways with God's will, where even our enemies are disarmed by His favor.

†

JUNE 17

When a man's ways please the Lord, He makes even his enemies to be at peace with him. (Proverbs 16:7)

Cultivate → God is the true peacemaker, and when we live to honor Him, He handles conflicts in ways we never could. Today, focus on one challenging relationship in your life and commit to praying for God's peace over it.

Then, take a practical step to demonstrate the grace of God in that relationship. It could be a kind word, a small act of service, or simply resisting the urge to engage in conflict. Trust that God is at work, even when you cannot see it.

"Lord, help me to walk in a way that pleases You. Teach me to trust You in my relationships, knowing that You are the One who brings true peace. Amen."

†

JUNE 18

This is my comfort in my affliction, for Your word has given me life. (Psalm 119:50)

Contemplate → From personal experience, I can testify that God's Word has been my comfort in the most uncomfortable situations. This *Psalm of Perseverance* is not an invitation to get comfortable in affliction—because that leads to complacency and self-pity. Rather, it is a declaration that God's Word sustains us, giving us life even in the face of adversity.

Affliction is often the place where God's promises become personal. His Word doesn't just inspire us—it breathes life into our brokenness, reviving what feels lost or weary. Pain can either paralyze you or propel you. For me, affliction became the fuel for my faith, and God's Word was the foundation that kept me standing when everything else felt like it was falling apart.

If you let it, your pain will push you toward purpose, and God's promises will be the lifeline that gives you strength to press on. His Word doesn't just lead you through affliction—it breathes life into your spirit so you can endure it with hope.

†

JUNE 19

This is my comfort in my affliction, for Your word has given me life. (Psalm 119:50)

Cultivate → God's Word is not just a source of encouragement—it is our lifeline. Even in hardship, His truth is our anchor, reminding us that affliction is temporary, but His promises are eternal.

Instead of dwelling on your struggles today, look outward. Reach out to someone who is facing difficulty and share a word of encouragement, whether through a text, call, or prayer. When we offer comfort to others, we are reminded of the comfort we ourselves have received.

"Lord, help me to take my eyes off my own struggles and be a source of encouragement to someone else today. Thank You for giving me life through Your Word. Amen."

†

JUNE 20

A man is not established by wickedness, but the root of the righteous cannot be moved. (Proverbs 12:3)

Contemplate → The root that runs deep and holds firm is the one anchored in Jesus Christ. A shallow foundation will crumble under pressure, but a life rooted in righteousness stands unshaken, no matter the storm. Even flowers, once trampled, instinctively turn back toward the sun. Likewise, when your faith is grounded in the Son, He will not allow you to be moved.

The deeper your roots go, the stronger you become. Wickedness may seem to prosper for a time, but it lacks stability—it withers without a lasting foundation. This *Proverb of Perseverance* reminds us that our strength comes not from outward success but from inward depth.

Stay at the feet of Jesus, dig deep into His truth, and you will stand firm.

†

JUNE 21

A man is not established by wickedness, but the root of the righteous cannot be moved. (Proverbs 12:3)

Cultivate → The deeper your roots, the stronger your resilience. Today, take a step to nourish your spiritual foundation. Whether it's through prayer, fasting, Scripture study, or quiet reflection, invest in strengthening your root system.

Find one area in your life that needs deeper spiritual grounding. Write down one commitment you will make this week to grow stronger in that area. Then, trust that God will establish you in righteousness.

"Lord, when I feel shaken, remind me to stay rooted in You. Strengthen my faith so I can rise again, knowing that Your righteousness keeps me grounded and unshakable. Help me trust in Your sustaining power through every storm. Amen."

†

JUNE 22

For His anger is but for a moment, His favor is for life; Weeping may endure for the night, but joy comes in the morning. (Psalm 30:5)

Contemplate → God's discipline is never without purpose. His correction lasts only for a moment, but His favor endures for a lifetime. Even in our hardest seasons, when darkness feels overwhelming and the night seems endless, we have the assurance that *morning will come*. Weeping may last through the night, but it does not last forever—God's joy always breaks through.

Like the Arctic Tern, which journeys through months of darkness in its polar migration yet continues flying toward the light, we are called to keep moving forward in faith—trusting that even the longest night cannot cancel God's sunrise.

This *Psalm of Perseverance* encourages us to press through seasons of struggle with the expectation that God's triumph will meet us on the other side. When the night feels long, hold on to His promise.

Your sorrow is temporary, but *His joy is eternal.*

†

JUNE 23

For His anger is but for a moment, His favor is for life; Weeping may endure for the night, but joy comes in the morning. (Psalm 30:5)

Cultivate → Seasons of darkness can feel overwhelming, but they are never permanent. Hold on to the promise that *God's joy is coming.* His timing may not align with ours, but His deliverance always arrives right on time.

Today, take a physical step of faith. Before you begin your day beyond this devotional, speak this verse aloud as a declaration of trust in God's timing. Let it be the reminder that joy is on the way. Then, as you step into your day, carry that promise with you—whether in moments of peace or seasons of uncertainty.

"Lord, even in my weeping, I trust You. I believe that joy is coming, and I will hold on to Your favor through every season. Thank You for being my light in the darkest nights, and for giving me strength to trust in Your timing. Amen."

†

JUNE 24

Do not be wise in your own eyes; Fear the Lord and depart from evil. It will be health to your flesh, and strength to your bones. (Proverbs 3:7-8)

Contemplate → Pride is a silent destroyer, convincing us that we have all the answers while leading us further from God's wisdom. This Proverb warns against trusting in our own understanding because human wisdom is limited, flawed, and often deceptive. Instead, true wisdom begins with fearing the Lord—having reverence for His authority and surrendering to His guidance.

Not only is this truth spiritual, but it is also physical. Living apart from God leads to stress, anxiety, and even physical illness. The weight of carrying everything alone weakens both the soul and body. But when we depart from evil and trust in the Lord, He strengthens us—inside and out.

There is health in humility and healing in surrender.

†

JUNE 25

Do not be wise in your own eyes; Fear the Lord and depart from evil. It will be health to your flesh, and strength to your bones. (Proverbs 3:7-8)

Cultivate → God's wisdom brings wholeness, while self-reliance leads to exhaustion. Where in your life are you depending on your own understanding instead of seeking God's wisdom? Ask Him to reveal any area where pride has kept you from fully trusting Him.

Today, make a shift. Instead of making a decision based on what seems right to you, pause and seek God's guidance first. Whether through prayer, Scripture, or godly counsel, let His wisdom lead your next step.

"Lord, I surrender my own wisdom to You. Teach me to trust in Your understanding, and strengthen me in body, mind, and spirit as I walk in obedience to You. Amen."

†

JUNE 26

Your word is a lamp to my feet and a light to my path.
(Psalm 119:105)

Contemplate → God's Word doesn't just inform—it illuminates. It serves as a lamp in the darkness, revealing the next step, and a light for the journey ahead, providing direction and clarity. Just as a lamp doesn't show the entire road at once, God often reveals only what we need for today, teaching us to walk by faith, not by sight.

In a world full of confusion and deception, His Word remains the only true guide. Without it, we stumble through life, making blind decisions and suffering unnecessary setbacks. But when we allow Scripture to light our way, we walk with purpose, confidence, and security.

His Word is the lamp—our job is to keep it lit. This requires more than occasional glances at Scripture; it demands a consistent relationship with His Word. Open your Bible daily, meditate on His truth, and allow His light to illuminate your steps. By staying close to His Word, you will never walk alone or without direction.

†

JUNE 27

Your word is a lamp to my feet and a light to my path. (Psalm 119:105)

Cultivate → God's Word is your daily guide, not just an occasional reference. Sometimes, His direction comes through Scripture, other times through the wisdom of godly counsel or the nudge of the Holy Spirit. But His light always shines for those who seek it.

Take a physical step today to symbolize your trust in His guidance. Go for a walk, even if just for a few minutes, and as you do, pray for God to direct your steps in a specific area of your life. Let the act of walking remind you that He is leading you forward, even if you can only see the next step.

"Lord, thank You for being the light that guides me. Teach me to trust Your Word as the foundation for every decision I make. Amen."

†

JUNE 28

He who earnestly seeks good finds favor, but trouble will come to him who seeks evil. (Proverbs 11:27)

Contemplate → Whatever you seek, you will find. This Proverb highlights a powerful truth: the direction of your pursuit determines the outcome of your life. When you earnestly seek good, you invite God's favor; but when you chase after what is wrong, trouble inevitably follows.

Seeking good is not a passive desire—it requires action. Just as a gardener doesn't hope for a harvest without first planting and tending the seeds, we must be intentional in pursuing righteousness. What you seek reveals what is in your heart, and what is in your heart shapes the path you walk.

God's favor is found when our hearts are set on what is right, true, and good.

†

JUNE 29

He who earnestly seeks good finds favor, but trouble will come to him who seeks evil. (Proverbs 11:27)

Cultivate → Seeking good is more than a thought—it's a pursuit. Living with intention requires actively looking for opportunities to bless others and reflect God's goodness.

Look for one way today to intentionally bring good into someone's life. It might be through an encouraging word, an act of kindness, or even choosing to extend grace instead of judgment. Sometimes seeking good means stepping out of your comfort zone—calling someone who's hurting, apologizing when you've been wrong, or going the extra mile when no one's watching.

Before the day ends, take action. Do something that reflects Christ's goodness, knowing that God's favor is found in those who live to reflect His heart.

"Lord, let my heart be fixed on seeking and doing good. Help me to plant seeds of kindness, truth, and love, knowing that in You, there is always a harvest of favor. Let my pursuit of good point others to You. Amen."

†

JUNE 30

A fire goes before Him, and burns up His enemies round about. His lightning's light the world; the earth sees and trembles. The mountains melt like wax at the presence of the Lord, at the presence of the Lord of the whole earth. (Psalm 97:3-5)

Contemplate → God's presence is unstoppable. This Psalm is a powerful reminder that our Lord is not weak or distant—He is a consuming fire, a force that shakes the earth and melts mountains like wax. When we walk with Him, we do not walk in fear but in victory.

So why do we so often let the challenges of life intimidate us? We see obstacles like immovable mountains, forgetting that at God's presence, even the most unshakable things dissolve. If He controls the forces of nature, what enemy, fear, or stronghold can stand against Him?

Our faith needs no greater assurance than this: God is not just beside us—He goes before us.

†

JULY 1

A fire goes before Him, and burns up His enemies round about. His lightning's light the world; the earth sees and trembles. The mountains melt like wax at the presence of the Lord, at the presence of the Lord of the whole earth. (Psalm 97:3-5)

Cultivate → Stand in awe of the power of God! When fear, doubt, or obstacles rise against you, take a moment to declare God's strength over your situation. Speak aloud: *"My God goes before me, and at His presence, every stronghold must melt away."*

If there's a specific fear or challenge looming over you, visualize it in light of this Psalm. What happens when it stands before God? Take courage, knowing that His power is greater than anything you face.

"Lord, Your presence melts mountains and burns away every opposition. Fill my heart with boldness, and remind me that I walk in the victory of Your power. No fear can stand against You. Amen."

†

JULY 2

The righteous man walks in his integrity; His children are blessed after him. (Proverbs 20:7)

Contemplate → Integrity is not just personal—it's generational. I love the word *integrity* because it instantly reminds me of my father. He didn't just preach this Proverb—he lived it. And because of his unwavering commitment to honor God, I firmly believe my brothers and I are blessed after him.

A righteous man's integrity is like a torch passed down from generation to generation. It lights the way, sets an example, and ensures that even when darkness tries to creep in, those who follow will never have to walk without direction. As we reflect on what it means to walk in righteousness, let us recognize that the choices we make today will impact our children, our families, and even our nation.

Stay faithful and undivided—it's the foundation your children will stand on and be provided for.

†

JULY 3

The righteous man walks in his integrity; His children are blessed after him. (Proverbs 20:7)

Cultivate → True freedom isn't found in lawlessness, but in integrity. As we celebrate Independence Day tomorrow, we reflect on the cost of freedom—both in our nation and in our faith. Just as integrity shapes families, it also shapes nations. The righteousness of one generation secures the blessings of the next.

Commit to one action this week that reflects godly integrity, knowing your example can impact others for generations. It may be standing for truth when it's unpopular, keeping your word when it's difficult, or leading with humility instead of pride.

Walk uprightly today to lay a foundation of blessings for those who follow.

"Lord, help me to walk in integrity, not just for myself, but for those who come after me. May my life reflect Your truth, so that my children and future generations may live in the freedom of Your righteousness. Amen."

†

JULY 4

When you walk, your steps will not be hindered, and when you run, you will not stumble. (Proverbs 4:12)

Contemplate → There's wisdom in the pace. Walking gives us time to see what's ahead, adjust our steps, and maintain balance. It's no coincidence that we call it a *Christian walk*—a steady journey of faith, one step at a time. When we walk with wisdom, our steps are unhindered, and we remain in control of our footing.

Running, however, is different. It requires more endurance, quicker reactions, and greater awareness of obstacles. Walking uphill requires slow, deliberate steps. Running downhill demands focus to avoid losing control. Both require wisdom to maintain balance.

And just as our nation celebrates its freedom today, we're reminded that true freedom isn't found in speed or strength—but in walking wisely under God's guidance. When wisdom leads the way, we can run without falling and walk without fear.

Wisdom applied propels, while wisdom denied fails. Move at God's pace, and you will never stumble.

†

JULY 5

When you walk, your steps will not be hindered, and when you run, you will not stumble. (Proverbs 4:12)

Cultivate → Every step matters. The choices we make each day shape the path we walk and the direction we run. When guided by God's wisdom, our steps are steady, and our purpose is clear. Are you walking in wisdom, or are you rushing ahead without direction?

Pause today and ask God to confirm your next step. Whether it's a decision you're facing, a goal you're pursuing, or a trial you're walking through, seek His wisdom before moving forward. Pray, listen, and trust that He will guide your feet.

"Lord, direct my steps today. Keep me from rushing ahead without Your wisdom, and steady my feet on the path You have set for me. I trust You to lead me where I need to go. Amen."

†

JULY 6

***If I say, "Surely the darkness shall fall on me," even the night shall be light about me; Indeed, the darkness shall not hide from You, but the night shines as the day; The darkness and the light are both alike to You.
(Psalm 139:11-12)***

Contemplate → God sees through the darkness. What we perceive as overwhelming, uncertain, or impenetrable is nothing to Him. Sometimes, it takes the dark for us to fully recognize our need for the true Light, Jesus Christ. Even when we feel consumed by darkness—whether through trial, grief, or confusion—God's presence never dims. He surrounds us with grace, even when we cannot see it.

Imagine being lost at sea, with nothing but darkness around you. Then, a lighthouse appears, its beam cutting through the blackness to guide you home. God's presence is that constant light—never fading, always leading. If we trust Him in the shadows, we will find that He is just as present in the night as He is in the day. Light and darkness are alike to Him. The only question is: Will we trust His vision over our own? It is better to wake up in dark circumstances with God's presence than to wake up in light without His assurance.

†

JULY 7

If I say, "Surely the darkness shall fall on me," even the night shall be light about me; Indeed, the darkness shall not hide from You, but the night shines as the day; The darkness and the light are both alike to You.
(Psalm 139:11-12)

Cultivate → Darkness cannot hide God's presence. No matter how uncertain or heavy a situation may seem, God's light is never outmatched. Think about one area in your life where things feel unclear, overwhelming, or uncertain. Instead of focusing on the darkness, shift your perspective—God already sees through it.

Tonight, before bed, turn off all the lights and sit in stillness for a few moments. Let the darkness around you remind you that even here, God is fully present. Then pray:

"God, thank You for being my light in the darkest moments. Help me trust Your presence, even when I can't see or understand the path ahead. Remind me that darkness is never dark to You, and give me the faith to rest in Your assurance, knowing You are always near, guiding me through. Amen."

†

Matthew Maher

PART V

OPPORTUNITY

Proverbs & Psalms That Lead, Direct, and Guide:
The SUPPORT That Paves The Way!

JULY 8

Commit your works to the Lord, and your thoughts will be established. (Proverbs 16:3)

Contemplate → This Proverb paves the way for everything we do. Whatever "work" you find yourself in—whether daily responsibilities, creative pursuits, or personal goals—when you offer it to God, He directs your thoughts and strengthens your steps.

Before writing this section, I prayed this very verse, giving my work to the Lord, and I am confident that He will establish it. Not because of my own efforts, but because I have chosen to let Him lead. Faith is trusting that God will pave the way, even when we cannot see the full path ahead. Like a tightrope walker relying on his balance pole, we must let God's Word stabilize us when life feels uncertain.

Have you given Him the lead in your work, your plans, and your purpose?

†

JULY 9

Commit your works to the Lord, and your thoughts will be established. (Proverbs 16:3)

Cultivate → Yesterday we reflected on committing our works to the Lord—but trust is more than a one-time prayer; it's a daily decision. Whether in your career, family, ministry, or personal ambitions, committing your work to God ensures that His wisdom shapes your thoughts, and His purpose guides your plans.

Today, before starting any task, pause and pray: *"Lord, I commit my work to You. Guide my hands, align my thoughts with Your will, and establish my steps. Let all I do bring glory to You. Amen."*

Then, take one intentional step toward fully trusting Him with your efforts, whether it's praying before a big decision, adjusting your plans to align with His Word, or simply working with excellence as an act of worship.

†

JULY 10

Lord, who may abide in Your tabernacle? Who may dwell in Your holy hill? He who walks uprightly, and works righteousness, and speaks the truth in his heart.
(Psalm 15:1-2)

Contemplate → This Psalm begins with a powerful question: *Who has the privilege to approach God, the Most High?* Who can dwell in His presence on His holy hill? The answer is clear—those who walk uprightly, work righteously, and speak truthfully.

This is not a call to perfection but a challenge to persist in pursuing a life of integrity. God isn't asking for flawlessness; He's calling us to a consistent walk of obedience and honesty. Walking uprightly means choosing what's right even when it's difficult. Working righteously is about serving others with integrity and compassion. Speaking truthfully requires both courage and humility, allowing our words to reflect what's true in our hearts.

Just as Jesus walked uprightly and spoke truth, may we follow His example in our daily lives. God elevates those who follow these principles, lifting them to His "holy hill." If you desire to abide in His presence, the opportunity is yours.

†

JULY 11

Lord, who may abide in Your tabernacle? Who may dwell in Your holy hill? He who walks uprightly, and works righteousness, and speaks the truth in his heart.
(Psalm 15:1-2)

Cultivate → Drawing near to God is a privilege, but it comes with a call to righteousness. This Psalm reminds us that living justly, working with integrity, and speaking truth is not just about actions, it's about the condition of the heart.

Examine your life today. *Is there an area where you need to be more upright, honest, or faithful?* Ask God to reveal where He wants to refine you and commit to making that change. Just as a sculptor chisels away excess stone to reveal a masterpiece, allow God to shape your heart into a reflection of His truth.

"Lord, search my heart and align my ways with Yours. Help me walk in integrity, work with righteousness, and speak truth in love. Draw me closer to You as I seek to dwell in Your presence. Amen."

†

JULY 12

Then you will walk safely in your way, and your foot will not stumble. (Proverbs 3:23)

Contemplate → How do we walk safely and avoid stumbling? By soaking in the wisdom of God's Word! Scripture provides the solid ground we need to navigate life's uncertainties. Instead of being drenched by life's stumbling storms, why not take the opportunity presented in Scripture to build a storm shelter?

Notice the certainty in this verse—it doesn't say, *"You may walk safely"* or *"Your foot may not stumble."* No! It boldly declares, *"You WILL walk safely"* and *"Your foot WILL NOT stumble."* Why such confidence? Because when you are anchored in God's Word, His wisdom guides your steps, providing stability and security.

A life submerged in the world will inevitably fall, but a life emerged in the Word will stand firm. Saturate yourself in His truth, and trust that His wisdom will lead you safely forward, step by step. When Scripture leads your steps, you will not slip.

†

JULY 13

Then you will walk safely in your way, and your foot will not stumble. (Proverbs 3:23)

Cultivate → Wisdom keeps your steps secure. The best way to walk safely through life is to ground yourself in God's Word. This is not a passive process but a daily commitment—an intentional anchoring in His truth. Each morning presents a new opportunity to place your feet firmly on the solid ground of Scripture.

Start today. Set aside time in the morning to read a passage from God's Word and reflect on how His wisdom can guide you throughout the day. Ask Him to guard your steps, guide your heart, and keep you from stumbling. And as you walk through the day, remember that safety is found in staying close to Him.

"Lord, lead me in Your wisdom. Secure my steps so that I may walk in Your truth, stand firm in faith, and follow the path You have prepared for me. Amen."

†

JULY 14

The Lord gives freedom to the prisoners.
(Psalm 146:7b)

Contemplate → A prisoner is someone held captive—whether mentally, physically, or spiritually. Yet true freedom is found only in the Lord Jesus. As Scripture declares, *"Where the Spirit of the Lord is, there is liberty"* (2 Corinthians 3:17).

Spiritual freedom isn't defined by our circumstances. Even when life feels confining—whether through hardship, regret, or limitation—God's freedom remains limitless. No chain, no wall, and no hardship can confine a soul that is set free by Christ.

The world offers a counterfeit version of freedom—temporary, fleeting, and often deceptive. But in Jesus, freedom is eternal. Even those in the darkest prison cells have sung songs of deliverance because their souls were unshackled in Him. His presence breaks every chain, lifts every burden, and leads us to lasting liberty.

†

JULY 15

The Lord gives freedom to the prisoners.
(Psalm 146:7b)

Cultivate → Freedom in Christ is unshakable. It exists beyond circumstances, chains, or struggles. Even when we feel bound—by fear, by sin, by trials—God's freedom remains.

Take a moment to thank the Lord for the freedoms He has secured in your life. Then, identify an area where you still feel spiritually or emotionally bound. Instead of carrying it alone, declare the freedom of Christ over it and surrender it to Him.

"Lord, thank You for the freedom You give, even in the midst of captivity. Teach me to walk in that liberty daily, trusting that Your truth always sets me free. Amen."

†

JULY 16

A merry heart does good, like medicine, but a broken spirit dries the bones. (Proverbs 17:22)

Contemplate → Joy is more than a feeling—it's a remedy. Like a dose of medicine that restores strength to a weary body, a merry heart refreshes the soul and sustains the spirit. Just as medicine fights infection or restores energy, joy combats negativity and nurtures hope.

In contrast, a broken spirit is like a drought in the desert—it drains vitality and leaves you dry, brittle, and weary. Bitterness acts like a slow poison, eroding strength from within and clouding every perspective.

Choosing joy is choosing health. A heart that finds reasons to smile—even in difficulty—acts as a prescription for perseverance. Laughter lifts the soul like fresh air filling the lungs. Gratitude energizes like sunlight breaking through storm clouds. The best doctor might say, *"Keep a merry heart—it's the medicine that never expires."*

†

JULY 17

A merry heart does good, like medicine, but a broken spirit dries the bones. (Proverbs 17:22)

Cultivate → As we learned yesterday, joy is more than an emotion—it's an intentional choice, a practice that refreshes the heart like medicine and strengthens the soul like exercise. Even in difficult moments, we can train ourselves to choose gratitude over gloom and laughter over lament.

Today, take a proactive step toward cultivating joy. Identify one situation that normally frustrates you—a traffic jam, a stressful task, or a difficult conversation—and intentionally approach it with a smile and a positive mindset. Rather than allowing negativity to take hold, speak life into that moment. Joy doesn't ignore hardship; it chooses to see God's hand beyond it.

"Lord, help me cultivate a merry heart. Teach me to find joy even in struggles, and let my spirit reflect Your goodness and grace. Strengthen me to choose joy as my response to life's challenges. Amen."

†

JULY 18

Examine me, O Lord, and prove me; Try my mind and my heart. (Psalm 26:2)

Contemplate → This verse presents a profound invitation—to willingly ask God to inspect the hidden corners of our hearts. It's one thing to admit our flaws, but it's another to courageously say, *"Lord, shine Your light into my life—test me, refine me, and reveal what needs to change."*

Much like sunlight streaming through a window reveals dust we didn't know was there, God's presence uncovers the unseen motives, attitudes, and desires that need His cleansing touch. It's uncomfortable at times, like standing in front of a mirror that exposes every blemish. Yet it's also necessary, for every test, every trial, and every refining fire is an opportunity for growth.

Think of it like gold being purified in the fire—the intense heat removes impurities, leaving behind something stronger, purer, and more valuable. Are you bold enough to invite His examination today, trusting that His refining hand will shape you for His glory?

†

JULY 19

Examine me, O Lord, and prove me; Try my mind and my heart. (Psalm 26:2)

Cultivate → Examination requires both surrender and action. Inviting God to search your heart is not a passive request—it's an intentional step toward transformation.

Today, find a quiet place where you can reflect without distraction. As you pray, ask the Lord to reveal anything in your heart that needs refining—a harmful habit, a lingering resentment, or a prideful attitude. If He brings something to light, don't push it aside. Instead, take one clear step toward change. Whether it's offering forgiveness, confessing sin, or seeking accountability, commit to moving forward.

Growth begins with awareness, but lasting change comes when we respond in obedience.

"Lord, I invite Your examination. Reveal anything in me that hinders my walk with You, and give me the strength to respond in faith. Shape my heart and mind to reflect Your truth. Amen."

†

JULY 20

But whoever listens to me will dwell safely, and will be secure, without fear of evil. (Proverbs 1:33)

Contemplate → Wisdom is always calling, but are we truly listening? Hearing is more than sound—it's about attention, intention, and response.

In ancient times, a city's security depended heavily on its gatekeepers. While towering walls provided defense, those stationed at the gate held the true power to guard or expose the city. Likewise, your ears and heart are the gateways to your spiritual life. What voices are you allowing in? Are you welcoming wisdom or entertaining anxiety, doubt, and deception?

If we fill our minds with noise, we risk drowning out the voice of God. But when we lean in to hear His wisdom, we secure our spiritual city—protected and unshaken.

Let your ear-gate welcome the sound of truth, the voice of peace, and the counsel of wisdom. When you listen to God, you will dwell securely, guarded from the threats that seek to invade your heart and mind.

†

JULY 21

But whoever listens to me will dwell safely, and will be secure, without fear of evil. (Proverbs 1:33)

Cultivate → Listening to God isn't just about hearing—it's about heeding His voice and walking in obedience. His wisdom is our stronghold, our refuge from confusion and fear. But just like a fortified city, we must be intentional about which voices we allow through the gate.

Today, pause and assess one voice, habit, or influence in your life—is it strengthening your faith or weakening your security in Christ? Ask yourself: *Does this draw me closer to God or distract me from Him?* If it doesn't align with His wisdom, make the intentional decision to shut the gate on it. True peace comes from choosing God's voice above all others and trusting that His way leads to life.

"Lord, help me to listen to Your wisdom above all else. Silence the voices that sow confusion, fear, or doubt, and guide me to walk securely in Your truth. I choose to trust Your voice today. Amen."

†

JULY 22

***I acknowledged my sin to You, and my iniquity I have not hidden. I said, "I will confess my transgressions to the Lord," and You forgave the iniquity of my sin.
(Psalm 32:5)***

Contemplate → Psalm 32 paints a powerful picture of the Lord's forgiveness—a cleansing flood that washes away what once weighed us down. Imagine trying to run a race while dragging a heavy chain. The longer you carry it, the more exhausted you become. Sin is like that chain—binding us in guilt, shame, and spiritual fatigue.

Confession is the key that unlocks that chain. David didn't try to justify, minimize, or hide his sin—he acknowledged it and surrendered it to the Lord. The result? Freedom. God's forgiveness is immediate and complete, yet we must take the first step.

You may feel unworthy of forgiveness, but His grace has already been paved for you. Don't let the weight of guilt keep you from running freely in the mercy God has already provided. Drop the chain, take the key, and walk forward in the freedom of His forgiveness.

†

JULY 23

I acknowledged my sin to You, and my iniquity I have not hidden. I said, "I will confess my transgressions to the Lord," and You forgave the iniquity of my sin.
(Psalm 32:5)

Cultivate → Confession is an act of trust, believing that God's mercy is greater than our mistakes. Instead of avoiding conviction, embrace it as an invitation to deeper freedom in Christ. The next time you feel the weight of guilt, don't run from it—bring it before the Lord immediately. He is not waiting to condemn but to restore.

Practice confessing regularly, rather than waiting until sin becomes a burden too heavy to carry. Make it a habit to examine your heart and surrender anything that stands between you and God's peace.

"Lord, give me the courage to confess quickly and completely, trusting in Your unfailing mercy. Thank You for forgiving me before I even ask. Help me walk in the joy of Your grace. Amen."

†

JULY 24

He who guards his mouth preserves his life, but he who opens wide his lips shall have destruction.
(Proverbs 13:3)

Contemplate → I once heard it said that a wise person is one who, when they have nothing worthy to say, doesn't give wordy evidence of the fact. There's power in restraint. Guarding your mouth isn't a sign of weakness—it's a mark of wisdom. Sometimes silence is the strongest statement you can make.

Picture your words like arrows in a quiver. Each one has the potential to hit a target or cause unnecessary harm. The wise person knows when to release an arrow and when to keep it secured. A fool, however, fires recklessly, unaware of the destruction their careless speech can bring.

What flows from your mouth reveals what's been stored in your heart. If you want to preserve your life and relationships, practice holding back when emotions run high. Restraint isn't retreat—it's the wisdom that protects and preserves. Sometimes, guarding your words is the greatest step forward you can take.

†

JULY 25

He who guards his mouth preserves his life, but he who opens wide his lips shall have destruction.
(Proverbs 13:3)

Cultivate → As we heard yesterday, words are like arrows—once released, they cannot be taken back. Practicing the discipline of silence is a powerful way to ensure your words hit the right mark.

Today, challenge yourself to pause before you speak—especially in moments of frustration, disagreement, or pride. Before responding, silently ask yourself: *Is what I'm about to say necessary, kind, and true?* If not, choose silence instead.

If a situation feels heated, try this: Take a deep breath and count to five before answering. This brief pause gives you space to filter your words through wisdom rather than emotion.

"Lord, help me to guard my tongue and use my words for good. Let my speech reflect wisdom, patience, and grace, bringing life to those who hear. Amen."

†

JULY 26

How can a young man cleanse his way? By taking heed according to Your word. (Psalm 119:9)

Contemplate → A heart saturated with God's Word is a life washed clean, even in a world stained by sin. This *Psalm of Opportunity* reveals that true cleansing isn't achieved through lip service or worldly advice—it comes from *heart service*, a deliberate commitment to following God's Word.

Many attempt to cleanse their own path through self-improvement or moral effort, but no amount of external washing can erase the stains within. Only God's Word has the power to purify the heart and renew the mind.

Heeding His Word means more than simply hearing it—it's absorbing it, applying it, and aligning your life with its truth. The more we soak in Scripture, the clearer our path becomes. So take heed—because it's God's Word that washes us white as snow.

†

JULY 27

How can a young man cleanse his way? By taking heed according to Your word. (Psalm 119:9)

Cultivate → There is a difference between merely *hearing* God's Word and *heeding* it, and that's application. God's truth isn't just meant to fill our minds—it's meant to guide our steps.

Today, take one intentional step to live out a biblical principle. Maybe that means choosing honesty when it's easier to hide the truth, offering forgiveness when resentment feels justified, or showing kindness where irritation could take hold. Each small step of obedience cleanses and strengthens your path.

To deepen this, commit to memorizing a verse that addresses an area where you need spiritual renewal. As His Word becomes rooted in your heart, it will transform your actions and purify your life.

"Lord, let Your Word cleanse my heart and guide my steps. Help me not only to hear it but to live it out, so that my life reflects Your truth and righteousness. Amen."

†

JULY 28

The way of the lord is strength for the upright, but destruction will come to the workers of iniquity.
(Proverbs 10:29)

Contemplate → The way of the Lord is not just a path—it's a fortress of strength for those who trust Him. Picture a sturdy lighthouse built on a rocky cliff. No matter how fierce the storm, the structure stands firm because its foundation is anchored in solid ground.

Similarly, when we walk in God's way, His strength surrounds and sustains us. Obedience to His Word acts like that firm foundation, keeping us secure when life's waves crash in.

Conversely, the "workers of iniquity" are like sailors who ignore the lighthouse's warning and steer toward shallow waters. The result is inevitable—a shipwreck of their own making.

God's way may not always seem easy, but it's always steady. His path shields, strengthens, and secures those who walk in it.

†

JULY 29

***The way of the lord is strength for the upright, but destruction will come to the workers of iniquity.
(Proverbs 10:29)***

Cultivate → Strength in the Lord is like an anchor in a raging storm—it holds firm when everything else feels unstable. But relying on His strength requires intentional steps. Where in your life are you feeling drained or overwhelmed? Perhaps it's in your prayer life, your relationships, or your ability to handle pressure.

Today, identify one area where you need to exchange your weakness for His strength. Instead of pushing forward in your own power, surrender that burden to God. Ask Him to strengthen you as you lean on His Word and rely on His presence.

True strength is not found in striving but in abiding—resting in the One who carries what we cannot.

"Lord, guide my steps to walk in Your way. Where I feel weak, be my strength. Keep me from the paths that lead to destruction, and uphold me in Your righteousness. Amen."

†

JULY 30

The Lord takes pleasure in those who fear Him, in those who hope in His mercy. (Psalm 147:11)

Contemplate → Does the Lord take pleasure in those with great wealth? In those with power? In those with human strength? No, no, and no! The Lord's delight is not found in worldly achievements but in the hearts that *reverence Him* and *trust in His mercy*.

To "fear" the Lord doesn't mean to shrink back in dread—it's to stand in reverent awe, recognizing that He alone holds ultimate authority. And to "hope in His mercy" is to confidently expect His kindness, even when we know we don't deserve it. The world tells us to put confidence in our own abilities, but this verse reminds us that what truly pleases God is our trust in Him, not in ourselves.

Our greatest offering isn't our achievements, possessions, or influence, it's a heart surrendered in reverence and anchored in the hope of His mercy.

†

JULY 31

The Lord takes pleasure in those who fear Him, in those who hope in His mercy. (Psalm 147:11)

Cultivate → If God takes pleasure in those who hope in Him, then hope itself is an act of worship. Instead of focusing on what you lack, fix your heart on His mercy. Take time to thank Him for His past faithfulness and remind yourself that His goodness hasn't run out.

What is one area where you need to place your hope back in God's mercy? A situation that feels out of control? A need for forgiveness? A desire for direction? Surrender it to Him, trusting that He delights in your faith.

"Lord, I place my hope in You, not in my own strength. Teach me to trust in Your mercy and walk in reverence before You. May my faith bring You pleasure, as I rest in Your goodness. Amen."

†

AUGUST 1

**Even a fool is counted wise when he holds his peace;
when he shuts his lips, he is considered perceptive.
(Proverbs 17:28)**

Contemplate → Wisdom isn't measured by how much you know but by how well you manage what you say. Even someone perceived as foolish can appear wise by practicing restraint. Perhaps in the past, you've struggled with impulsive words—blurting out frustrations or over-explaining yourself. Yet this Proverb reveals a hopeful truth: silence can redeem what speech may have damaged.

Choosing silence doesn't mean you've lost your voice, it means you've gained control. When you hold your peace, you reflect strength, not weakness. Like a calm captain steering a ship through turbulent waters, a quiet response often reveals deeper wisdom than a loud reaction.

Today, let silence be your ally—not to avoid truth, but to ensure your words are chosen with wisdom.

†

AUGUST 2

Even a fool is counted wise when he holds his peace; when he shuts his lips, he is considered perceptive.
(Proverbs 17:28)

Cultivate → Restraint is a form of wisdom that speaks louder than hasty words. The next time you're tempted to respond out of frustration or pride, pause. Silence isn't avoidance—it's allowing space for God's peace to settle the moment.

Before you speak, ask: *Am I adding value or venting emotion?* A well-timed pause allows room for God's wisdom to guide your words.

Today, practice the power of the pause. Whether in a tense conversation or when responding to criticism, take a breath, say a silent prayer, and choose words that reflect wisdom rather than reaction.

"Lord, teach me to guard my tongue and to pause before speaking. Help me reflect Your wisdom, responding with grace instead of impulsiveness. Amen."

†

AUGUST 3

Delight yourself in the Lord, and He shall give you the desires of your heart. (Psalm 37:4)

Contemplate → This verse isn't a promise that God will fulfill every want—it's a reminder that when we delight in Him, our desires are transformed to align with His. Like a compass adjusting to true north, our hearts are recalibrated as we seek His presence.

The desires He fulfills aren't always about what we get—they're about who we become. When you delight in the Lord, He plants His purpose in your heart like seeds in fertile soil—growing passions, dreams, and burdens that reflect His will.

Instead of asking, "*What do I want from God?*" ask, "*What does God want for me?*" As you delight in Him, trust that He will shape your desires to match His perfect plan.

†

AUGUST 4

Delight yourself in the Lord, and He shall give you the desires of your heart. (Psalm 37:4)

Cultivate → Many read this Scripture and assume it means God will grant any desire we have. Instead, it reveals how *He transforms our desires* to align with His will. As we grow in Him, our hearts begin to long for what He longs for.

Take time to reflect: How has God changed your desires over time? Have you seen Him remove selfish ambitions or sinful cravings and replace them with a hunger for righteousness? Thank Him for shaping your heart to reflect His own.

"Lord, I delight in You and trust that You are shaping my desires to match Your perfect will. Continue to mold my heart, so that I long for what pleases You above all else. Amen."

†

AUGUST 5

A soft answer turns away wrath, but a harsh word stirs up anger. (Proverbs 15:1)

Contemplate → When provoked, it's tempting to meet hostility with hostility. Even when we don't intend to escalate a situation, our reaction can become the spark that ignites the fire. Often, it's not just what we say, but how we say it that shapes the outcome.

This Proverb reminds us that "a soft answer" has the power to diffuse tension and redirect conflict. Softness isn't weakness; it's wisdom in action. It's a steady hand guiding a ship through rough waters—keeping calm when the storm rises.

Gentleness should shape more than just our words, it should influence our tone, posture, and presence. Harshness fuels anger like gasoline to a flame, but a calm, measured response becomes a firebreak—propping the situation up with peace instead of pulling it into chaos. When faced with tension today, let your soft answer become a steady bridge toward resolution.

†

AUGUST 6

A soft answer turns away wrath, but a harsh word stirs up anger. (Proverbs 15:1)

Cultivate → The next time you feel tension rising, pause before responding. Ask yourself: *Will my words escalate or defuse the situation?* Challenge yourself to respond with a soft answer, even if the other person doesn't.

Consider Jesus—He often faced hostility yet responded with wisdom and grace. His silence before His accusers, His gentleness with sinners, and His patience with His disciples all show the power of a soft answer. If the Son of God chose humility in the face of wrath, how much more should we?

When you feel the urge to react sharply today, take a deep breath, pray for wisdom, and let your words reflect the peace of Christ. A single soft response can shift the atmosphere and bring healing where anger could have caused damage.

"Lord, give me wisdom to speak with grace. Help me resist reacting in anger and instead reflect Your peace. Let my words be a testimony of Your love. Amen."

†

AUGUST 7

It is God who arms me with strength, and makes my way perfect. He makes my feet like the feet of deer, and sets me on my high places. (Psalm 18:32-33)

Contemplate → Who equips us for the valley lows? *It is God.* Who clears the path ahead of us? *It is God.* Who stabilizes our steps when the ground feels unsteady? *It is God.* And who lifts us to mountain highs? Still, *it is God.*

This Psalm paints a powerful picture of God's guidance and strength. Just as a deer effortlessly scales rugged terrain with balance and precision, God enables us to move forward with steady steps—even on uncertain ground. Deer don't hesitate or panic when crossing steep slopes; they are equipped for the climb. Likewise, God equips us to navigate life's highs and lows with confidence.

The path may be rocky, but His strength steadies our footing. Every challenge is an opportunity for God to demonstrate that He is the One who arms, strengthens, and leads us upward. Trust Him—He alone makes your way secure.

†

AUGUST 8

It is God who arms me with strength, and makes my way perfect. He makes my feet like the feet of deer, and sets me on my high places. (Psalm 18:32-33)

Cultivate → Stability in life comes from dependence on God, not our own strength. No matter what challenges you face, He has equipped you to stand firm. Like the feet of a deer, your footing is sure when you trust in His guidance. Even when the path is steep, He is leading you to higher places.

Take a walk today—whether around your neighborhood, at a park, or simply in a quiet space. With each step, reflect on how God is establishing your way. As you move, pray for His strength to keep you steady through every season of life.

"Lord, thank You for strengthening me and guiding my steps. Help me trust in Your stability rather than my own, knowing that You are leading me to the heights You have prepared for me. Amen."

†

AUGUST 9

***As iron sharpens iron, so a man sharpens the
countenance of his friend. (Proverbs 27:17)***

Contemplate → Character sharpening begins with interaction. Whether it's *sandpaper people* who rub you the wrong way or *frictional friends* who smooth you the right way, both are opportunities for growth.

This well-known Proverb reminds us that even the "hard rocks" of life can become the building *ProPs* of who we are becoming. Without friction, iron remains dull. Likewise, without godly relationships, our character risks becoming stagnant.

True sharpening happens when we engage with others who challenge us—those who speak truth in love, correct us when needed, and encourage us to grow. The process may feel uncomfortable at times, but like iron striking iron, the sparks are part of the refining process.

Embrace those who sharpen you and intentionally seek to be a sharpening force for others. Growth thrives in the grind.

†

AUGUST 10

As iron sharpens iron, so a man sharpens the countenance of his friend. (Proverbs 27:17)

Cultivate → God designed us for connection and accountability. Healthy relationships strengthen us, but they also expose areas where we need refining. *Who in your life challenges you to grow in Christ? Who helps sharpen your faith?*

Reach out to a friend or mentor who has been an iron-sharpening influence in your life. Thank them for their role in your spiritual journey, and if you haven't already, ask how you can be a source of encouragement for them as well.

"Lord, help me to surround myself with those who sharpen my faith and draw me closer to You. Let me be an encouragement to others, that together we may grow stronger in Your wisdom and purpose. Amen."

†

AUGUST 11

Search me, O God, and know my heart; Try me, and know my anxieties; And see if there is any wicked way in me, and lead me in the way everlasting.
(Psalm 139:23-24)

Contemplate → *"Search me, try me, and know me,"* we pray—but are we prepared for what God reveals? Asking for His inspection is one thing; embracing what He uncovers is another.

God's searchlight pierces deeper than we can see ourselves. Like a gardener digging beneath the surface to uproot hidden weeds, God reveals the sins, motives, and anxieties that we've tucked away. What He exposes may be uncomfortable, but it's always for our good.

David's prayer in this Psalm is not casual, it's courageous. It's a call for God to invade every corner of our heart, uncovering what hinders us from walking in His way. True transformation starts when we stop hiding and invite Him to cleanse and lead us.

Today, don't just pray the words—embrace the process. Trust that what He reveals, He will also heal.

†

AUGUST 12

Search me, O God, and know my heart; Try me, and know my anxieties; And see if there is any wicked way in me, and lead me in the way everlasting.
(Psalm 139:23-24)

Cultivate → A heart truly surrendered to God welcomes His refining work. When we ask Him to search us, we must also be ready to listen and respond.

Set aside ten minutes of uninterrupted time in prayer today, specifically asking God to search your heart. As He reveals areas that need realignment, write them down. Then, take one intentional step to address what He shows you—whether through repentance, forgiveness, or a commitment to walk in obedience.

"Lord, I invite You to search my heart. Show me anything that hinders my walk with You, and give me the strength to surrender it fully. Lead me in Your way everlasting. Amen."

†

AUGUST 13

A man's gift makes room for him and brings him before great men. (Proverbs 18:16)

Contemplate → God equips each of us with unique gifts, designed not only to bless us but to bless others. Like a key fitting perfectly into a lock, our God-given abilities "*make room*" for us in places we could never force our way into by human effort alone.

When we view our talents as divine assignments rather than personal achievements, we begin to see that our influence is God's doing. He opens doors, positions us in the right places, and connects us with the right people—not for self-promotion, but to reflect His goodness and advance His purposes.

Your gift is not just about what you do; it's about how you steward it. Faithfully use what God has given you, and trust that in His perfect timing, He will place you exactly where He intends—turning your gift into an opportunity to glorify Him.

†

AUGUST 14

A man's gift makes room for him and brings him before great men. (Proverbs 18:16)

Cultivate → Yesterday's reflection revealed how our God-given gifts act like a key, unlocking opportunities we could never create on our own. But here's the key's counterpart: a key is only effective when carried with intention.

Today, commit to actively using your gift. Identify one specific talent or strength God has given you, and ask yourself: *How can I put this to work today for His glory?* Whether it's speaking life into someone's situation, serving in a way that reflects His love, or creating something that inspires others, put your gift in motion.

God doesn't bless passive potential—He blesses faithful stewardship. As you take action, trust that He is aligning your steps, positioning you in places where your gift will reflect His goodness.

"Lord, thank You for the gifts You've entrusted to me. Help me to walk boldly in them today—not for my glory, but for Yours. Open the right doors, and may every opportunity point back to You. Amen."

†

AUGUST 15

I am the Lord your God, who brought you out of the land of Egypt; Open your mouth wide, and I will fill it. (Psalm 81:10)

Contemplate → In Scripture, "the land of Egypt" symbolizes bondage, captivity, and the crushing weight of sin. Yet God didn't just deliver His people from slavery—He led them into a place of provision and promise. Deliverance is never meant to leave us empty; it positions us to be filled.

This verse reminds us that God frees us not only from sin's grip but also for something greater—to receive His goodness. But here's the key: *we must respond.* The invitation to "open your mouth wide" speaks of a posture of faith—one that expects God to provide abundantly.

Imagine a baby bird in the nest, mouth stretched wide, completely dependent on its parent to fill it. In the same way, we must come before God with that same trust and hunger. He doesn't offer partial provision or minimal mercy—He overflows when we extend ourselves in faith.

Don't settle for scraps when God is ready to satisfy. Open wide, trust boldly, and be filled.

†

AUGUST 16

I am the Lord your God, who brought you out of the land of Egypt; Open your mouth wide, and I will fill it. (Psalm 81:10)

Cultivate → God's provision is never in short supply, but we often limit what we receive by playing it safe—keeping our hearts guarded, our prayers small, or our steps timid. Faith doesn't flourish in half-measures; it thrives when we "open wide" and invite God to fill every empty space.

What's one area in your life where you've been holding back—where doubt or fear has kept you from trusting God completely? Maybe it's your finances, a relationship, or a dream He's placed on your heart.

Today, take a bold step of faith. Identify that area, then open your heart in prayer and surrender. Ask God to fill what you've been hesitant to release, trusting that His provision will exceed your expectations.

"Lord, You have delivered me from bondage and called me to trust You fully. I open my heart, my life, and my faith to You—fill me with Your presence, Your wisdom, and Your provision. Amen."

✝

AUGUST 17

Train up a child in the way he should go, and when he is old he will not depart from it. (Proverbs 22:6)

Contemplate → This Proverb highlights both the responsibility and privilege of guiding children in the ways of the Lord. To *"train up a child"* is more than just instruction—it's intentional formation.

Like a gardener shaping a young tree, raising children requires patience, care, and consistency. A tree that bends early will grow crooked unless corrected, but with proper support, it will stand tall and strong.

Similarly, faith is taught through action and example. Training a child in truth is less about rules and more about relationship—walking alongside them like a parent teaching a child to ride a bike. There may be wobbles and falls, but steady guidance leads to stability and confidence.

Parents, mentors, and spiritual leaders are vital in propping up the next generation. Investing in their spiritual growth today plants seeds that will bear fruit for years to come—and for eternity.

†

AUGUST 18

Train up a child in the way he should go, and when he is old he will not depart from it. (Proverbs 22:6)

Cultivate → Words alone won't disciple the next generation—consistent action and example will. *Who in your life is watching how you live out your faith?*

This week, be intentional in modeling a godly principle—whether through prayer, serving others, showing integrity, or exercising patience. Then, take a moment to explain the *why* behind your actions to a child, teen, or younger believer. When they see faith in action, it plants seeds that take root and grow.

"Lord, help me be a faithful example to the next generation. May my actions reflect Your truth, and may I plant seeds of faith that will grow deep and remain strong. Use me to guide and encourage others in Your way. Amen."

†

AUGUST 19

A good man leaves an inheritance to his children's children, but the wealth of the sinner is stored up for the righteous. (Proverbs 13:22)

Contemplate → What will you leave behind? *Everything.* Not one possession will follow you into eternity. This Proverb reminds us that a "good man" thinks beyond his own lifetime and invests in generations to come.

Think of your legacy like building a bridge—a structure that spans generations, allowing those who follow to cross safely over the struggles and pitfalls you've faced. A true inheritance isn't measured in money but in the wisdom, faith, and values that guide others long after you're gone.

Earthly riches crumble, but a bridge of righteousness stands firm. Our grandchildren deserve a path paved with truth—one that time cannot erode and that leads directly to Christ. What you leave behind spiritually will carry more lasting weight than anything you leave behind materially.

†

AUGUST 20

A good man leaves an inheritance to his children's children, but the wealth of the sinner is stored up for the righteous. (Proverbs 13:22)

Cultivate → Just as a bridge connects one generation to the next, your legacy is built through intentional steps of faith. The greatest inheritance isn't wealth—it's the foundation of truth, character, and devotion to Christ that stands the test of time.

This week, build a "bridge of blessing" for the next generation. Identify one way you can actively pass down your faith—perhaps by writing a heartfelt letter of encouragement filled with Scripture, starting a family prayer tradition, or sharing a personal testimony that reveals God's faithfulness.

A legacy that points to Christ is the kind that future generations will stand on with confidence. Start building today.

"Lord, let my life be a bridge that leads others to You. Help me pass down the wisdom, faith, and truth that will guide future generations in Your way. Amen."

†

AUGUST 21

A good man deals graciously and lends; He will guide his affairs with discretion. Surely he will never be shaken; the righteous will be in everlasting remembrance. (Psalm 112:5-6)

Contemplate → Generosity is like planting trees you may never sit under—its impact extends far beyond what you can see. A good man gives not only from his wallet but from his heart, offering grace, wisdom, and kindness. Yet, he doesn't give recklessly; he *"guides his affairs with discretion,"* ensuring his generosity is intentional and Spirit-led.

A gracious giver knows that giving isn't about loss—it's about planting seeds that will bear fruit long after they're gone. When we give with wisdom, we invest in something that outlives us—a legacy of righteousness. The world may see generosity as risky, but Scripture assures us that those who give graciously will *"never be shaken."*

Why? Because their security isn't tied to wealth—it's anchored in God's faithfulness. When you give with purpose, you're not just meeting needs; you're building shade for generations to come. The righteous are remembered not for what they hoarded, but for what they gave away.

†

AUGUST 22

A good man deals graciously and lends; He will guide his affairs with discretion. Surely he will never be shaken; the righteous will be in everlasting remembrance. (Psalm 112:5-6)

Cultivate → Generosity guided by wisdom leaves a lasting impact. Yesterday's reflection reminded us that true giving isn't reckless—it's intentional and Spirit-led. Today, consider one area where you can practice thoughtful generosity.

Whether it's offering financial help to someone in need, encouraging a struggling friend, or giving your time to serve, let your generosity be purposeful. And if possible, give quietly, seeking no recognition—only to reflect God's kindness.

"Lord, help me to give graciously, walk in wisdom, and trust in Your provision. May my generosity reflect Your love and leave a legacy of faith that honors You. Amen."

†

AUGUST 23

Whenever I am afraid, I will trust in You.
(Psalm 56:3)

Contemplate → Fear has a way of convincing us that we're alone, yet Scripture reminds us that trust is the antidote. Fear isn't always loud—it often whispers doubt, feeds anxiety, and distorts our view of reality. But David's words in this Psalm reveal that trusting God isn't just a feeling; it's a decision.

When fear rises, trust steps in to silence the lies. Trust says, *"God is still in control."* Trust says, *"I am not alone."* Trust says, *"This moment doesn't define my future."* Just as David replaced his fear with faith, we too must choose to anchor our hearts in God's promises. Fear may attempt to shake us, but trust steadies our steps.

The next time fear sneaks in, don't suppress it—speak to it. Say aloud, *"Whenever I am afraid, I will trust in You."* Fear may knock, but faith must answer.

†

AUGUST 24

Whenever I am afraid, I will trust in You.
(Psalm 56:3)

Cultivate → Fear is a natural response, but faith is a supernatural choice. Fear can paralyze us, cloud our judgment, and make our problems seem larger than God's promises. But faith chooses to trust, even in the midst of uncertainty. Trusting in God doesn't mean we won't feel fear—it means we won't be ruled by it.

Think of one fear or uncertainty that has been weighing on you and then speak this verse aloud as a declaration of faith. Whenever that fear resurfaces, replace it with trust by repeating this verse and remembering that God is always greater than the circumstances before you.

"Lord, I give my fears to You. Strengthen my trust and remind me that You are my refuge. Help me to walk in faith, knowing that You are in control. Amen."

†

Matthew Maher

PART VI

RESTORATION

Proverbs & Psalms That Amend & Restore:
The SUPPORT That Rebuilds The Right
Foundation!

AUGUST 25

Who satisfies your mouth with good things, so that your youth is renewed like the eagle's. (Psalm 103:5)

Contemplate → Eagles are known for their strength and renewal, soaring higher than any other bird. This Psalm reminds us that God Himself is the one who restores and satisfies us, giving us renewed energy when we feel weak or weary. Just as an eagle molts its feathers and emerges stronger, we too experience spiritual renewal when we seek our satisfaction in the Lord rather than in temporary pleasures.

It's easy to feel depleted by the demands of life, but God desires to fill us with His goodness—not just physically but spiritually. *Are you looking to the right source for renewal?* The world offers momentary relief, but only God provides lasting strength and satisfaction.

When we hunger for Him, He fills us with what truly revives and sustains our souls.

†

AUGUST 26

Who satisfies your mouth with good things, so that your youth is renewed like the eagle's. (Psalm 103:5)

Cultivate → God alone renews and strengthens us, filling our lives with good things that satisfy far beyond anything the world offers. His restoration isn't just physical—it is spiritual, emotional, and mental. When we allow Him to fill us, we experience renewal like the soaring eagle, rising above the weight of exhaustion and discouragement.

Think of someone in your life who may feel drained or discouraged. How can you be an encouragement to them? Whether through a word of affirmation, a small act of kindness, or simply praying for them, seek to reflect God's renewal in their life. As you pour into others, trust that God will also refresh your own spirit, reminding you that true strength comes from Him alone.

"Lord, You are my source of renewal and strength. Fill me with what truly satisfies, and help me to encourage others who need Your refreshing presence. Let me be a vessel of Your love, lifting up those who are weary as You continue to renew my own spirit. Amen."

†

AUGUST 27

A man will be satisfied with the good by the fruit of his mouth, and the recompense of a man's hands will be rendered to him. (Proverbs 12:14)

Contemplate → The words we speak and the work we do have lasting effects. This Proverb teaches us that satisfaction comes when we speak wisely and labor diligently, for both our words and our efforts are like seeds sown into the world.

The way we speak and act is a reflection of what is inside of us. A fruitful mouth brings nourishment, and hands that work with diligence reap rewards. Consider the words you speak daily—do they build others up or tear them down? Are your hands engaged in work that reflects godliness?

God's principle is clear: what we put out into the world will, in time, come back to us.

†

AUGUST 28

A man will be satisfied with the good by the fruit of his mouth, and the recompense of a man's hands will be rendered to him. (Proverbs 12:14)

Cultivate → Words and actions are like seeds—what we plant, we eventually harvest. This Proverb reminds us that when we speak words of life and work diligently with our hands, we will reap satisfaction and goodness. The impact of what we say and do not only shapes the lives of those around us but also returns to us in ways we often don't expect.

Be intentional this week. Speak encouragement and kindness to at least one person each day, making a conscious effort to use your words for good. Look for opportunities to serve someone with your hands—whether through an act of generosity, helping with a task, or offering comfort. As you pour into others, trust that God will return the fruit of your goodness, bringing fulfillment and joy to your own life.

"Lord, may my words be fruitful and my hands be faithful in service. Help me to sow goodness into the lives of others, trusting that You will satisfy my heart in return. Amen."

†

AUGUST 29

May He grant you according to your heart's desire, and fulfill all your purpose. (Psalm 20:4)

Contemplate → Have you ever seen a sailboat drift aimlessly because its sails weren't positioned properly? No matter how strong the wind blows, a misaligned sail won't carry the boat toward its destination. Similarly, this *Psalm of Restoration* reveals that God's fulfillment comes when our hearts are aligned with His will.

Many people chase their desires only to find themselves stranded in disappointment, like a boat spinning in circles. But when we seek God's kingdom first, He fills our sails with purpose, propelling us forward in ways we never imagined. His purpose is not just about what we accomplish—it's about who we become in the process.

Ask yourself: Are your sails aligned with His wind, or are you drifting on your own? True fulfillment is found when your desires are steered by His direction.

†

AUGUST 30

May He grant you according to your heart's desire, and fulfill all your purpose. (Psalm 20:4)

Cultivate → Fulfillment isn't about chasing your own ambitions—it's about letting God steer your course. If you've been feeling stuck or aimless, it may be time to adjust your sails.

Spend time in prayer today asking, *"Lord, what direction are You guiding me in this season?"* Then, take one intentional step toward that prompting—whether it's starting a new habit, reconnecting with someone, or stepping into an opportunity you've been hesitant about.

Just as a boat moves only when the sails are positioned correctly, your heart must be surrendered to His direction for true purpose to unfold. Trust Him to guide you forward.

"Lord, I surrender my desires to You. Align my heart with Your will and steer me toward the purpose You have planned. May I move with Your wind and find fulfillment in following Your lead. Amen."

†

AUGUST 31

A good name is to be chosen rather than great riches, loving favor rather than silver and gold.
(Proverbs 22:1)

Contemplate → A name is more than a title—it's a living testimony. Think of your name as a signature you leave behind wherever you go. Some signatures are remembered for wisdom, kindness, and faithfulness, while others are tied to betrayal or selfish gain.

Proverbs reminds us that a name built on integrity is more valuable than wealth. Money can be spent or stolen, but a good name—once damaged—is hard to reclaim. However, the power of redemption cannot be overlooked. Through Christ, even a tarnished name can be restored and rewritten with grace and new purpose.

Every day you're writing a story with your words, actions, and decisions. The question is: What kind of signature are you leaving behind?

†

SEPTEMBER 1

A good name is to be chosen rather than great riches, loving favor rather than silver and gold.
(Proverbs 22:1)

Cultivate → Like a signature on a check, your name carries weight—it either inspires trust or causes doubt. Today, consider what your name means to those around you. Are your words reliable? Are your actions consistent with godly character?

Commit to one act of integrity this week that strengthens your reputation. Whether it's keeping your word, taking responsibility, or humbly asking forgiveness, let your choices reflect Christ's influence.

If past mistakes have stained your name, trust that God's grace is greater. He restores, renews, and reclaims what's been broken. Walk in integrity, and trust Him to rewrite your story.

"Lord, let my name reflect Your truth. Teach me to walk uprightly, honoring You with my words and actions. May my life leave a lasting testimony of faithfulness. Amen."

†

SEPTEMBER 2

The Lord upholds all who fall, and raises up all who are bowed down. (Psalm 145:14)

Contemplate → Falling is inevitable, but staying down is a choice. Picture a child learning to walk—each stumble isn't final because loving hands are always ready to lift them back up. That's how God deals with His children. He doesn't just watch us fall—He reaches out to steady us, to pull us back to our feet.

But there's a condition—He raises those who are *"bowed down."* Humility is key. To be bowed down is to admit our need, to acknowledge that we can't stand without Him. The world may say, *"Pick yourself up,"* but Scripture reveals that true restoration comes when we surrender and allow God to lift us.

No failure is final in the hands of a faithful Father. The question isn't whether He's willing to lift you—it's whether you're willing to let Him.

†

SEPTEMBER 3

The Lord upholds all who fall, and raises up all who are bowed down. (Psalm 145:14)

Cultivate → Just as a child learning to walk relies on the steady hand of a parent, God's hand is there to steady us when we stumble. Think back to a time when He lifted you out of failure, grief, or discouragement. How did His grace meet you in that moment?

Now, look around. Is there someone in your life who feels weighed down? Reach out today—whether with a kind word, a listening ear, or a simple prayer—and remind them that God's hand is still reaching out. Just as He upheld you, be a vessel of His comfort and strength for someone else.

"Lord, thank You for steadying me when I fall. Help me extend Your grace to those who are weary and burdened. Use me as a reminder that no one falls beyond Your reach. Amen."

†

SEPTEMBER 4

For the ways of man are before the eyes of the Lord, and He ponders all his paths. (Proverbs 5:21)

Contemplate → God's gaze is never distracted. While we may forget the details of our own lives, He sees everything with perfect clarity. Consider how a watchmaker inspects every delicate gear and spring inside a timepiece—each part matters because every movement affects the whole.

In the same way, the Lord examines not only what we do but *why* we do it. His watchful eye isn't cold or distant—it's the loving gaze of a Father who longs to see His children walk wisely. This truth should bring both comfort and caution. Comfort, because He knows our hidden struggles and quiet victories. Caution, because no path is concealed from His sight.

If God carefully ponders our steps, shouldn't we thoughtfully consider where our feet are headed?

†

SEPTEMBER 5

For the ways of man are before the eyes of the Lord, and He ponders all his paths. (Proverbs 5:21)

Cultivate → Since God weighs every step we take, we should pause and examine our own path. Ask yourself: *Am I walking in alignment with His will?* If there's a choice you've been avoiding or a direction you've been hesitant to pursue, now is the time to bring it before Him.

Pray for clarity, then take one intentional step toward obedience—whether it's reconciling a strained relationship, adjusting your priorities, or aligning your words with truth. Remember, just as a watchmaker fine-tunes each gear to keep time perfectly, trust that God's guidance will refine your steps to bring peace and purpose.

"Lord, You see my every step. Reveal where I need to change direction, and give me courage to follow Your lead. Help me trust that Your wisdom keeps my path secure. Amen."

†

SEPTEMBER 6

__Create in me a clean heart, O God, and renew a steadfast spirit within me. Do not cast me away from Your presence, and do not take Your Holy Spirit from me. (Psalm 51:10-11)__

Contemplate → David's plea in this Psalm reveals a heart desperate for more than forgiveness—it longs for transformation. He doesn't simply ask God to clean up his mess; he asks for a brand-new heart. The word "create" (bara) is the same word used in Genesis 1:1, meaning to create from nothing. David knew his heart wasn't just broken—it was bankrupt. He needed God to start over, to form something entirely new within him.

This prayer goes beyond seeking relief from guilt—it's a cry for closeness with God. David feared the thought of being separated from His presence more than he feared the consequences of his sin. That's the mark of true repentance—not just sorrow for what's been done, but a hunger to be restored in fellowship with God. If you've ever felt distant from God, know this: He is still near. And when we humbly ask Him to renew our hearts, He doesn't merely patch the cracks—He crafts something new, pure, and strong.

†

SEPTEMBER 7

Create in me a clean heart, O God, and renew a steadfast spirit within me. Do not cast me away from Your presence, and do not take Your Holy Spirit from me. (Psalm 51:10-11)

Cultivate → Restoration starts within, and when God renews our hearts, it naturally overflows to others. Today, instead of asking God to fix circumstances, ask Him to renew your heart. Bring before Him any bitterness, selfishness, or apathy you've been holding on to.

Then, let that renewal extend outward. Identify one person who may be discouraged, burdened, or distant from God. Pray for them, and then reach out with a simple act of kindness—whether it's a text, a phone call, or a thoughtful gesture. Sometimes, God uses renewed hearts to renew others.

"Lord, create a clean heart within me, and renew my spirit with strength and steadfastness. Help me to reflect Your love to those in need, that they too may experience the renewal only You can bring. Amen."

†

SEPTEMBER 8

He who keeps instruction is in the way of life, but he who refuses correction goes astray. (Proverbs 10:17)

Contemplate → Instruction isn't just about gaining knowledge—it's about transformation. Staying on the *"way of life"* requires more than hearing truth; it requires humbly accepting correction.

Think about a GPS. When you make a wrong turn, it doesn't stay silent—it corrects your path. Ignoring those directions doesn't erase the mistake; it only takes you further off course. Likewise, when God provides correction through His Word, His Spirit, or wise counsel, He's not trying to shame us—He's redirecting us back to the path of life.

The challenge isn't whether God corrects us—it's whether we're willing to listen. The wise understand that correction is not rejection; it's a course adjustment that spares us from destruction. Will you take heed, or keep ignoring the signs?

†

SEPTEMBER 9

He who keeps instruction is in the way of life, but he who refuses correction goes astray. (Proverbs 10:17)

Cultivate → Correction is like a compass—it points us back to where we need to be. Today, reflect on an area of your life where you've resisted correction. It could be a habit, a relationship, or an attitude. Ask God to reveal where He's trying to redirect you.

Then take action. Whether it's seeking guidance from a trusted mentor, asking forgiveness, or adjusting a behavior, choose to respond to His correction with humility. Remember, correction isn't condemnation, it's an invitation to walk in the way of life.

"Lord, thank You for Your loving correction. Help me embrace the guidance You provide, trusting that every course adjustment is designed to lead me closer to Your purpose. Amen."

†

SEPTEMBER 10

Draw near to my soul, and redeem it; Deliver me because of my enemies. (Psalm 69:18)

Contemplate → Ever felt like you were drowning in your struggles—unable to catch your breath? This verse is David's desperate cry for God to draw near, not only to defend him but to redeem his soul. The physical battles he faced mirrored the deeper spiritual turmoil within him.

This Psalm is also prophetic, pointing to Jesus—the One who endured betrayal, mockery, and abandonment. On the cross, Christ felt the suffocating weight of separation yet trusted the Father's nearness. His suffering secured our redemption, proving that no matter how overwhelmed we feel, God is always within reach.

Like a lifeguard diving into raging waters, God doesn't just observe our distress—He steps in to rescue us. When life feels like it's pulling you under, cry out to Him, and He will draw near to save.

†

SEPTEMBER 11

Draw near to my soul, and redeem it; Deliver me because of my enemies. (Psalm 69:18)

Cultivate → On this day of remembrance, we reflect on moments of crisis—both personal and national. Tragedy reveals our deep need for God's nearness, not just for external rescue but for inner healing and redemption.

Today, invite God to draw near to the burdens you carry. Whether it's grief, fear, or uncertainty, take a moment in prayer, worship, or quiet reflection. Let Him meet you in that place. Then, consider reaching out to someone who may be struggling—a friend, neighbor, or family member—and offer a listening ear or encouraging word.

"Lord, draw near to my soul and redeem me in moments of distress. Heal the wounds I carry, and deliver me from anything that seeks to pull me away from You. Let Your presence restore and sustain me, and may I never forget that true security is found in You alone. Amen."

†

SEPTEMBER 12

The refining pot is for silver and furnace for gold, but the Lord tests the hearts. (Proverbs 17:3)

Contemplate → The Lord desires to see His reflection in us, and it is through the refining process of faith that our hearts are purified and come forth as gold or silver—Christ-like in character. Just as metals must be placed in fire to remove impurities, our faith is tested through trials that reveal the depths of our hearts.

Often, it is only through struggle that our true character is shaped and strengthened. The trials we endure are not meant to destroy us but to refine us, drawing out what is pure and holy while burning away the excess that hinders our spiritual growth.

The refiner knows the process is complete when He can see His reflection in the finished product. Likewise, God longs to see His Son in us, shining brightly through the refining fire of His grace.

†

SEPTEMBER 13

The refining pot is for silver and furnace for gold, but the Lord tests the hearts. (Proverbs 17:3)

Cultivate → Every trial has a purpose, and every hardship can lead to refinement when surrendered to God. Think of a sculptor chiseling away at stone—the process may seem harsh, but every strike is intentional, revealing the beauty beneath. Likewise, God's refining fire is designed to shape you into His image.

What challenge are you currently facing that might be part of His refining process? Instead of resisting, choose to trust that He is using this season to purify your heart and strengthen your faith.

Consider one way you can embrace God's refining work—whether by responding with patience in adversity, forgiving when it's difficult, or standing firm in faith despite uncertainty. Like the sculptor's chisel revealing the masterpiece within, let your actions reflect His presence in you.

"Lord, I trust You in the refining process. Though the fire may be uncomfortable, I know You are using it to purify my heart. Help me endure with faith, so that I may reflect Your love, grace, and righteousness in all I do. Amen."

†

SEPTEMBER 14

For He spoke, and it was done; He commanded, and it stood fast. (Psalm 33:9)

Contemplate → This *Psalm of Restoration* declares the power of God's spoken word. From creation to redemption, He speaks, and it comes to pass. The same voice that called the universe into existence is the same voice that upholds it.

Imagine an artist painting a masterpiece—every stroke intentional, each detail purposeful. Yet, even if someone were to vandalize the painting, the artist has the power to restore it. In the same way, humanity often dismantles what God has beautifully crafted, yet nothing we break is beyond His ability to restore.

When God speaks, nothing can stand against His will. What He commands remains unwavering—"*and it stood fast.*" Time does not weaken His decrees, nor does failure nullify His power. If His Word is strong enough to sustain creation, it is certainly strong enough to sustain us. No matter what seems lost or impossible, His spoken word remains the final authority over all things.

†

SEPTEMBER 15

For He spoke, and it was done; He commanded, and it stood fast. (Psalm 33:9)

Cultivate → Like a skilled artist restoring a vandalized masterpiece, God can rebuild what has been damaged in your life. Consider an area where you feel things have crumbled or fallen apart. Instead of dwelling on the brokenness, declare the truth of God's spoken Word over it. His Word has the power to restore, rebuild, and renew what seems lost.

Find a Bible verse that speaks to your situation and memorize it. Speak it aloud today as a reminder that God's power is greater than your circumstance. Just as an artist brings life back to a defaced painting, God can restore what feels shattered in your life.

"Lord, Your Word is unshakable, and Your promises never fail. Speak into my life, restore what is broken, and help me trust that Your commands will stand firm forever. Amen."

†

SEPTEMBER 16

A merry heart makes a cheerful countenance, but by the sorrow of the heart the spirit is broken.
(Proverbs 15:13)

Contemplate → The condition of your heart affects far more than just your emotions—it shapes your outward demeanor and even your spiritual health. Think of your heart like a lantern. When joy fuels its flame, it illuminates your face, your attitude, and your interactions. But when sorrow is left unchecked, it's as if that flame has dimmed, casting a shadow over everything.

This Proverb reminds us that joy is not dictated by circumstances. You have a choice: to cultivate joy or to allow sorrow to overtake you. Life will always bring hardships, but joy anchored in Christ transforms even the darkest seasons. A cheerful heart is not naïve to pain; rather, it finds strength in God's promises.

Lasting joy does not come from fleeting pleasures but from a heart rooted in Christ. His presence is the ultimate source of a cheerful countenance and an unbreakable spirit. What is the mood of your heart today? Is your lantern burning brightly, or does it need fresh oil from His presence?

†

SEPTEMBER 17

A merry heart makes a cheerful countenance, but by the sorrow of the heart the spirit is broken.
(Proverbs 15:13)

Cultivate → Just as a flame spreads when it touches another wick, joy multiplies when you share it. The more you give it away, the more it grows within you. This week, commit to intentionally bringing joy to others—whether through encouragement, a thoughtful act, or simply a genuine smile. Watch how this not only brightens someone else's day but also rekindles your own joy.

To keep your "lantern" burning, keep a gratitude journal and record one moment each day where you brought joy to someone or where someone's joy impacted you.

"Lord, fill my heart with Your joy so that it may overflow into the lives of those around me. Help me to reflect Your light, even in difficult moments, and to find strength in the joy that comes from You alone. Amen."

†

SEPTEMBER 18

Restore us, O God; Cause Your face to shine, and we shall be saved! (Psalm 80:3)

Contemplate → True restoration goes deeper than simply fixing what's broken—it's about being made whole in God's presence. This Psalm cries out for God's favor to return, for His face to shine upon His people once more. When His face shines on us, it's more than a symbol of blessing—it's the warmth of His nearness, a reminder that His presence brings life.

Restoration isn't a surface repair; it's a rebuilding from the inside out. God doesn't just patch wounds; He heals them completely. The Israelites cried for deliverance, but their greatest need wasn't just physical relief—it was spiritual renewal.

When life feels distant and fragmented, longing for God's restoration is the first step toward experiencing it. As we turn our faces toward Him in repentance and trust, we'll discover His face has already been turned toward us, shining with grace, ready to renew, revive, and restore.

†

SEPTEMBER 19

Restore us, O God; Cause Your face to shine, and we shall be saved! (Psalm 80:3)

Cultivate → Restoration in Christ is more than a second chance—it's a complete renewal of our hearts, minds, and spirits. Think back to a time when God restored something in your life—a relationship, a season of wandering, or a personal struggle. Let His past faithfulness strengthen your trust in His ongoing work.

Now, consider an area in your life that still needs His restoring touch. Bring it before Him in prayer, asking Him to shine His face upon it. Then take a practical step toward restoration—whether by reaching out to mend a relationship, rededicating time to God's Word, or offering gratitude for what He's already renewed.

"Lord, thank You for being the God of restoration. Shine Your face upon me and revive any area of my life that needs renewal. Help me walk in the fullness of Your saving grace, knowing that in You, I am made whole. Amen."

†

SEPTEMBER 20

Anxiety in the heart of man causes depression, but a good word makes it glad. (Proverbs 12:25)

Contemplate → Anxiety is like a weight pressing down on the heart—slowly tightening its grip until hope feels out of reach. It clouds our vision, trapping us in cycles of fear and uncertainty. Left unchecked, this burden can settle into discouragement, exhaustion, and eventually depression.

But God offers a powerful remedy—a good word. Just as the morning sun melts away lingering fog, an encouraging word has the power to cut through anxiety's haze. A reminder of God's promises, an uplifting message from a friend, or even speaking Scripture over your own life can restore clarity and renew hope.

We are called to both receive and give these life-giving words. By receiving encouragement, our hearts are lifted. By offering encouragement, we become part of God's plan to push back the weight of anxiety in someone else's life. Words have the power to restore, uplift, and heal—so let's choose to speak life.

†

SEPTEMBER 21

Anxiety in the heart of man causes depression, but a good word makes it glad. (Proverbs 12:25)

Cultivate → When anxiety knocks on the door of your heart, answer it with God's truth. Take an active step in replacing fear with faith by speaking Scripture over your worries. Find a verse that combats anxiety—perhaps Philippians 4:6-7 or Isaiah 41:10—and declare it aloud when stress arises.

Then, become a bearer of "good words." Reach out to someone today—a text message, a handwritten note, or a simple conversation can be the very thing that lifts their burden. You may never know how much your encouragement meant, but God does—and He multiplies the impact.

"Lord, when anxiety tries to pull me down, help me remember the power of a good word. Fill my heart with Your truth, and let my words be an encouragement to others. Thank You for the joy that comes from trusting in You. Amen."

†

SEPTEMBER 22

Unless the Lord has been my help, my soul would soon have settled in silence. If I say, "My foot slips," Your mercy, O Lord, will hold me up. (Psalm 94:17-18)

Contemplate → The world offers many things to lean on, but only one foundation can truly hold us up—God's unfailing mercy. Without Him, we fall. Without His help, our souls settle into silence, burdened by regret, shame, or hopelessness.

This verse reminds us that it's not about *if* we slip, but *when*. We are human, prone to stumbling, yet God does not abandon us in our weakness. The moment we cry out, "My foot slips," He is already there, catching us with His mercy and setting us back on solid ground.

The psalmist acknowledges a powerful truth: without God's help, we would remain stuck in our failures. But with His hand upholding us, we can rise again. Instead of being defined by our past missteps, we are strengthened by His unwavering grace. Our testimony is not about how many times we've slipped, but about how many times He has lifted us up.

†

SEPTEMBER 23

Unless the Lord has been my help, my soul would soon have settled in silence. If I say, "My foot slips," Your mercy, O Lord, will hold me up. (Psalm 94:17-18)

Cultivate → God's mercy is not just about picking us up when we fall—it's about teaching us how to walk in His strength. Instead of focusing on your failures, shift your mindset to how He has faithfully carried you through. Look back on a moment when you thought you had fallen too far, yet He lifted you. Write down how God's mercy brought you through it, and then share your testimony with someone who might need that encouragement.

Sharing our struggles and victories glorifies God and strengthens others. If you don't know who to share with, ask God to show you. Whether through a conversation, a text, or even a journal entry shared later, let His faithfulness be known.

"Lord, I praise You for never letting me settle in silence. Your mercy lifts me, and Your grace sustains me. Help me to be bold in sharing how You've carried me, that others may see Your goodness and trust in You as well. Amen."

†

SEPTEMBER 24

The generous soul will be made rich, and he who waters will also be watered himself. (Proverbs 11:25)

Contemplate → Generosity is not about what you have—it's about how you use it. Some of the wealthiest people are bankrupt in spirit because they hoard what they've been given, while some of the most generous have little in material possessions but overflow with joy. This Proverb reveals a divine principle: those who pour out are never left empty.

The metaphor of "watering" speaks to refreshing and nourishing others. When we intentionally give—whether through resources, encouragement, time, or service—we open ourselves to be replenished by God.

Our souls are enriched when we live with open hands, trusting that God is the source of all provision. Just as a well that continues to pour out fresh water never runs dry, a generous spirit is continually sustained by the Lord.

†

SEPTEMBER 25

The generous soul will be made rich, and he who waters will also be watered himself. (Proverbs 11:25)

Cultivate → Generosity isn't just about money—it's about mindset. Look for an opportunity this week to "water" someone's life. Maybe it's through your words—offering encouragement to someone who's struggling. Perhaps it's through your time—helping a friend or family member in need. Or it could be through small acts of kindness—buying someone a meal, sending a thoughtful message, or simply listening.

As you step out in generosity, reflect on how God refreshes your spirit in return. Keep a journal of the ways you bless others this week and how you see His provision and joy flow back into your life.

"Lord, help me to give with a cheerful heart, knowing that You are my provider. Teach me to water the lives of those around me and trust that You will replenish me in ways only You can. May my generosity reflect Your abundant love. Amen."

†

SEPTEMBER 26

But as for me, I will walk in my integrity; Redeem me and be merciful to me. (Psalm 26:11)

Contemplate → Integrity is often tested when no one's watching. The path of compromise may seem easier, yet David's declaration—*"But as for me"*—reveals a steadfast resolve to remain faithful, no matter what others chose to do.

Walking in integrity is like rowing against the current. The world's tide may push you toward compromise, but those committed to God's truth keep moving upstream. David's confidence wasn't in his own strength but in God's mercy and redemption. Integrity isn't perfection—it's consistency. Even when you stumble, choosing to return to God's path keeps your integrity intact.

When culture bends and values shift, will you stand with conviction and say, *"But as for me."*

†

SEPTEMBER 27

But as for me, I will walk in my integrity; Redeem me and be merciful to me. (Psalm 26:11)

Cultivate → Integrity doesn't happen by accident—it's built through intentional choices. Identify one area where compromise tries to creep in—whether in your words, your work, or your relationships.

Today, write your own *"But as for me"* statement—a personal declaration that defines how you will live for Christ. Place it somewhere visible as a reminder that integrity isn't shaped by popular opinion but by your unwavering commitment to God's truth.

"Lord, strengthen me to walk in integrity, even when it's difficult. Help me to stand firm in my convictions, trusting that Your mercy will uphold me when I falter. May my life reflect my devotion to You and Your mercy."

†

SEPTEMBER 28

He also brought me up out of a horrible pit, out of the miry clay, and set my feet upon a rock and established my steps. (Psalm 40:2)

Contemplate → Life's pits can feel like quicksand—the harder you struggle, the deeper you sink. Whether it's failure, grief, addiction, or regret, these moments often leave us feeling stuck, unsure if we'll ever stand on solid ground again.

Joseph knew this feeling well. Betrayed by his brothers and thrown into a pit, he had no control over what would happen next. Yet God wasn't absent in that pit—He was positioning Joseph for something greater. When Joseph's feet were sinking in mud, God was already preparing to place them on stone. Years later, Joseph stood on the *"rock"* of God's purpose, elevated to a place of influence in Egypt where he would save countless lives.

Like Joseph, you may feel stuck in a pit today, but God's plan doesn't end there. The same God who lifted Joseph out of a hopeless situation is ready to lift you, too—placing you on solid ground and guiding your steps toward His greater purpose.

†

SEPTEMBER 29

He also brought me up out of a horrible pit, out of the miry clay, and set my feet upon a rock and established my steps. (Psalm 40:2)

Cultivate → When Joseph was trapped in the pit, he had no idea that God was already preparing his path to the palace. What feels like a setback today may actually be God positioning you for something far greater.

Reflect on a time when God rescued you from hardship. What blessings, growth, or opportunities followed that deliverance? Write it down as a testimony of His faithfulness.

If you're in a pit right now, resist the urge to believe this is your final chapter. Ask God to guide your next step—whether it's seeking wise counsel, forgiving someone, or committing to daily prayer. Remember, the pit is never the end of the story when God is writing it.

"Lord, just as You lifted Joseph from the pit and established his steps, I trust You to do the same in my life. Lead me toward the purpose You've prepared for me, and help me to trust Your timing. Amen."

†

SEPTEMBER 30

Do not say, "I will recompense evil,"; Wait for the Lord, and He will save you. (Proverbs 20:22)

Contemplate → Revenge feels natural—but it's never moral. When someone wrongs us, the impulse to strike back can be overwhelming. Yet Proverbs reminds us that vengeance is not our job; it's God's.

Acting in retaliation only deepens our wounds. Like tugging on a thorn lodged in our skin, we may feel justified in the moment, but we risk driving the pain deeper. *Waiting on the Lord*, however, is an act of faith. It means trusting that He sees what we cannot and will handle injustice in His perfect way and time.

Choosing patience isn't passivity—it's releasing the burden of bitterness and trusting God's wisdom over our own impulses. Let go of the desire to settle the score and watch how God's justice always proves better than our own.

†

OCTOBER 1

Do not say, "I will recompense evil,"; Wait for the Lord, and He will save you. (Proverbs 20:22)

Cultivate → Waiting doesn't mean doing nothing—it means trusting while choosing grace. When you're tempted to retaliate, pause and pray: *"Lord, I trust You with this."*

As a practical step, write down any grievances or offenses you've been holding on to. Then, symbolically release them—tear the paper, burn it, or place it in your Bible as a reminder that the matter is now in God's hands.

If you feel led, go a step further: respond to the person who wronged you with an unexpected act of kindness. A patient word, a sincere prayer for them, or even quiet restraint can be a powerful way to break the cycle of hurt.

"Father, when I'm tempted to take matters into my own hands, remind me that Your justice is always perfect. Help me trust You enough to wait, and fill my heart with the peace that comes from knowing You will save. Amen."

†

OCTOBER 2

Many are the afflictions of the righteous, but the Lord delivers him out of them all. (Psalm 34:19)

Contemplate → Following God doesn't exempt us from hardship—it often invites it. The righteous walk isn't a detour around affliction but a path that passes directly through it. Yet affliction is never the final word.

Shadrach, Meshach, and Abed-Nego stood firm in faith and still found themselves thrown into the fire (Daniel 3). But instead of being consumed, they were accompanied—by the very presence of God. Likewise, Daniel's integrity led him into a den of lions, but God shut their mouths (Daniel 6). Deliverance doesn't always mean avoiding the fire—it means God stands with us in it.

Like gold refined in the flames or clay shaped under pressure, our afflictions are tools in God's hands—designed to strengthen, refine, and prepare us for His purpose. The question isn't *if* hardship will come, but *who* we will trust to carry us through it.

No matter what trial you're facing today, trust that the God who walked in the furnace and silenced the lions is walking with you now.

†

OCTOBER 3

Many are the afflictions of the righteous, but the Lord delivers him out of them all. (Psalm 34:19)

Cultivate → Just as God shows up in our afflictions, He often sends others to walk with us through them. Think of someone facing a trial right now—whether grief, uncertainty, or hardship.

This week, reach out to them intentionally. Send a message, offer to pray, or share a Scripture that has encouraged you. Sometimes, your presence can be the very reminder they need that God's deliverance is already at work.

"Lord, when affliction comes, help me trust that You are with me in the fire. Strengthen my heart and use me to encourage others who are facing trials of their own. May my words and actions point to Your faithful deliverance. Amen."

†

OCTOBER 4

Do not remove the ancient landmark, nor enter the fields of the fatherless; For their Redeemer is mighty; He will plead their cause against you.
(Proverbs 23:10-11)

Contemplate → In ancient Israel, boundary stones marked property lines, symbolizing family inheritance and God-ordained order. To move one was theft—a quiet but calculated act of injustice. For the fatherless, whose earthly protectors were gone, this crime was especially cruel. Yet this Proverb reveals a powerful truth: *Their Redeemer is mighty.*

Today, boundary stones of truth and morality are under constant attack. The world attempts to redraw the lines God has firmly set—redefining right and wrong, blurring the boundaries of faith, and distorting His Word. But just as God defends the fatherless, He stands as the mighty Guardian of truth.

When culture shifts and compromise tempts, stand firm. Don't let the world redefine what God has already established. His justice prevails, and His redemption is sure.

†

OCTOBER 5

Do not remove the ancient landmark, nor enter the fields of the fatherless; For their Redeemer is mighty; He will plead their cause against you.
(Proverbs 23:10-11)

Cultivate → Just as God defends the fatherless, He calls us to uphold the boundaries He has set. Where do you see His landmarks under attack—in your family, your church, or your community?

This week, take one intentional step to defend what is right. Speak truth in love where confusion reigns. Encourage someone who feels spiritually "fatherless" and vulnerable. Stand firm in conversations where God's design is being challenged.

By standing for His truth, you reflect the heart of our Redeemer—the One who defends, restores, and upholds what the world tries to erase.

"Lord, give me the courage to stand firm in Your truth. Help me be a voice of encouragement and a reflection of Your justice. May my life point to You, the ultimate Defender and Redeemer. Amen."

†

OCTOBER 6

He calms the storm, so that its waves are still.
(Psalm 107:29)

Contemplate → Whether God allows the storm or commands it, He controls it. Life's voyage can feel smooth for a season, but when we begin steering by self-reliance or ambition, He may allow turbulent waves to shake us awake.

Storms aren't random—they're revealing. Like sailors forced to toss excess cargo overboard to stay afloat, we sometimes lose possessions, comforts, or false securities so that we can rediscover our dependence on Him. The storm strips away what cannot sustain us, making room for what truly can.

Other times, the storm exposes where we've anchored our faith—whether in our own plans, resources, or strength. The waves will not be stilled until we stop striving and surrender to His sovereignty.

If the storm feels relentless, remember this: its motion is not meaningless. It's a call to realign your course with His perfect plan—the one that leads to still waters.

†

OCTOBER 7

He calms the storm, so that its waves are still.
(Psalm 107:29)

Cultivate → Storms test where we place our trust. Are you gripping the wheel, trying to steer through the chaos on your own? Or are you willing to let God take control?

Today, instead of praying for the storm to end, ask God what He's revealing through it. Then take one intentional step toward trusting Him—whether by identifying something you've been clinging to tightly and releasing it to Him, or by sharing your burden with a trusted friend or mentor who can pray with you.

As sailors secure their anchor before the winds rage, you too must anchor your heart in His Word. Trust that in His time, He will calm the waves.

"Lord, I release my fears and uncertainties to You. Help me trust Your purpose in the storm and rest in the peace that only You provide. Align my heart with Your will and still the waves in Your perfect time. Amen."

†

OCTOBER 8

__Wisdom has built her house, she has hewn out her seven pillars. (Proverbs 9:1)__

Contemplate → Wisdom is not built in haste; it's constructed with intention. Just as a skilled craftsman carefully selects each beam and stone, wisdom requires deliberate choices that strengthen our character and deepen our understanding.

The "seven pillars" in this Proverb symbolize completeness—a life supported by spiritual maturity, integrity, and discernment. A house without strong pillars is vulnerable to collapse, no matter how impressive its outward appearance.

Likewise, a life lacking wisdom may seem stable for a time, but when pressure comes, its foundation is exposed. God's wisdom is the framework that keeps us steady and secure, reinforcing what's weak and bringing strength to what is strong.

Ask yourself: Are you building your life with wisdom—or patching it together with shortcuts and opinions? A life constructed on God's truth will endure every storm.

†

OCTOBER 9

Wisdom has built her house, she has hewn out her seven pillars. (Proverbs 9:1)

Cultivate → Wisdom starts with the Word of God. One of the best ways to build a foundation of wisdom is by memorizing Scripture so that truth is embedded in your heart before you even need it.

Choose one verse from Proverbs (perhaps this one) and commit to memorizing it today. Write it on a notecard or make it your phone's wallpaper. Say it out loud as you make your way through your day. As you meditate on it, ask God to show you how to apply it in daily life.

"Lord, help me to build my life on the foundation of Your wisdom. Let Your truth fill my heart and guide my steps. Strengthen my character with discernment and understanding, so I may be firmly rooted in Your Word. Establish my thoughts, my choices, and my actions in Your wisdom. Amen."

†

Matthew Maher

PART VII

THANKFULNESS

Proverbs & Psalms That Express Gratitude:
The SUPPORT That Sustains Contentment!

OCTOBER 10

I lay down and slept; I awoke, for the Lord sustained me. (Psalm 3:5)

Contemplate → Sleep is one of life's greatest reminders that we are not in control. No matter how determined or independent we are, sleep forces us to surrender. Each night, our bodies shut down, our minds drift into unconsciousness, and for hours, we have no awareness or power over what happens around us. Yet, each morning we wake—not because we sustained ourselves, but because God did.

Imagine a pilot who guides a plane through turbulence, only to hand control over to the autopilot for the night flight. While passengers rest in their seats, unaware of the unseen navigation, the autopilot maintains direction. Likewise, when we rest, God's sustaining hand quietly secures our path, guarding us even when we are most vulnerable.

This verse reveals the rhythm of dependence: *"I lay down" (I surrender); "and slept" (He grants me peace); "I awoke" (He revives me); "for the Lord sustained me" (He alone keeps me safe).* Each new morning is not just a reset—it's a reminder that His hand never let's go.

†

OCTOBER 11

I lay down and slept; I awoke, for the Lord sustained me. (Psalm 3:5)

Cultivate → Rest is an act of trust. Just as a child sleeps soundly because they know their parents are near, we are called to rest in the confidence that God is watching over us.

This week, try turning bedtime into an opportunity for surrender. Each night, take captive the thoughts, anxieties, or burdens weighing you down. Then, in prayer, release them to God—one by one. Picture yourself handing each concern to Him, trusting that He sustains you as you sleep.

If anxious thoughts return during the night, quietly repeat this verse as a declaration of trust: *"I lay down and slept; I awoke, for the Lord sustained me."*

"Lord, I lay my burdens before You, trusting that You sustain me even when I am unaware. Thank You for each new morning You give. Help me to rest in Your peace, knowing You hold my life in Your hands. Amen."

†

OCTOBER 12

For whom the Lord loves He corrects, just as a father the son in whom he delights. (Proverbs 3:12)

Contemplate → Discipline isn't rejection—it's refinement. I remember telling my fellow inmates during my time of incarceration that we were blessed beyond measure—because God only corrects those He loves. The loss of freedom we faced wasn't merely the result of poor choices; it was also a sign of God's relentless pursuit.

Like a loving father who intervenes when his child veers off course, God's correction is designed to protect and restore us. A parent who ignores their child's destructive behavior isn't showing love—they're displaying neglect. In contrast, God's correction is active love in motion. He steps in—not to destroy, but to develop us.

Correction may sting in the moment, but it's the hand of a Father at work, shaping us for something greater. His discipline isn't about shame—it's about sharpening. It chisels away pride, softens hardened hearts, and strengthens what was once weak. When we see correction through this lens, we recognize that it's not punishment—it's preparation.

†

OCTOBER 13

For whom the Lord loves He corrects, just as a father the son in whom he delights. (Proverbs 3:12)

Cultivate → Discipline often reveals the areas where we've resisted God's guidance. Today, reflect on one area where you've repeatedly faced hardship or correction. Is there a lesson God is teaching you that you've been reluctant to receive?

Instead of resisting, invite God to reshape you in that area. As a tangible step, write a prayer of surrender. Confess where you've struggled to embrace His correction and ask for the courage to walk in His wisdom. Keep this prayer in your Bible as a reminder that God's discipline is His love in action—working not against you, but for you.

"Lord, I acknowledge Your discipline as an act of love. Help me to embrace correction with a teachable heart, knowing You are shaping me for something greater. Align my steps with Your wisdom and lead me in the way everlasting. Amen."

†

OCTOBER 14

It is good for me that I have been afflicted, that I may learn Your statutes. (Psalm 119:71)

Contemplate → Affliction often feels like a storm—loud, chaotic, and unsettling. It disrupts our comfort, shakes our security, and sometimes leaves behind what feels like wreckage. Yet storms, while destructive, can also be revealing. When the winds die down, what's left standing proves to be the strongest and most secure.

In my life, affliction did just that. It tore down my pride, stripped away false comforts, and revealed the only thing that couldn't be shaken—God's Word. The storm that threatened to ruin me instead became the very thing that redirected me back to Him.

Looking back, I can say with confidence: *"It is good for me that I have been afflicted."* Why? Because it taught me to anchor my life on God's unshakable truth. When storms come—and they will—it's the foundation of His Word that keeps us standing.

†

OCTOBER 15

It is good for me that I have been afflicted, that I may learn Your statutes. (Psalm 119:71)

Cultivate → Storms may leave scars, but they also leave stories. Think back to a season when God brought you through difficulty. What did He teach you? How did He strengthen your faith?

This week, identify someone facing a storm of their own. Reach out with words of encouragement, sharing how God sustained you through your own season of hardship. If possible, offer a practical act of support—a listening ear, a prayer, or even a reminder from Scripture. Your story could be the anchor that helps someone else hold on.

"Lord, thank You for the lessons You teach me in the storms of life. Help me to trust that even in affliction, You are working for my good. Use my experiences to encourage others and point them to Your unfailing love. Amen."

†

OCTOBER 16

There is one who makes himself rich, yet has nothing;
And one who makes himself poor, yet has great riches.
(Proverbs 13:7)

Contemplate → Wealth is not always what it seems. Picture a man clutching a bag of fool's gold—glittering yet worthless. He thinks he's rich, yet his treasure holds no real value. Meanwhile, another man willingly lays down his last possession, yet finds himself surrounded by true riches—peace, contentment, and God's favor.

This Proverb reminds us that worldly wealth can be deceptive. The pursuit of status, power, and possessions often leaves us empty, yet surrendering these things can lead to true abundance. Jesus said, *"Blessed are the poor in spirit, for theirs is the kingdom of heaven."* To be "poor in spirit" is to let go of self-reliance and embrace our dependence on God.

The question is not how much you have, but what you're holding onto. Are you clinging to fool's gold or trusting in the true riches of Christ?

†

OCTOBER 17

There is one who makes himself rich, yet has nothing;
And one who makes himself poor, yet has great riches.
(Proverbs 13:7)

Cultivate → Sometimes, the greatest act of faith is choosing to let go. Ask yourself: *What am I clinging to that's robbing me of true peace and security?*

This week, take a deliberate step to *"make yourself poor."* That could mean surrendering control of a situation, forgiving a debt owed to you, or giving generously where it feels inconvenient. Trust that as you empty your hands, God will fill your heart with His peace and provision.

"Lord, I release my grip on the things that leave me empty. Teach me to trust in Your true riches, finding joy and contentment in Your presence alone. Amen."

†

OCTOBER 18

The day is Yours, the night also is Yours; You have prepared the light and the sun. You have set all the borders of the earth; You have made summer and winter. (Psalm 74:16-17)

Contemplate → Seasons remind us that change is inevitable, yet purposeful. Consider the life of a tree. In summer, its branches are full and flourishing, basking in the warmth of the sun. But as winter approaches, the tree surrenders its leaves, appearing lifeless and bare. Yet beneath the surface, the roots are strengthening, digging deeper into the earth to prepare for spring's renewal.

Our lives follow a similar rhythm. The bright "summer" seasons bring joy and clarity, while the dark "winter" seasons test our endurance and faith. Yet God is the Lord of both—present in our victories and our valleys. The same God who commands the rising sun also governs the setting night. The season you're in is not random—it's refining you, strengthening your roots, and preparing you for what's next.

The day belongs to Him. The night belongs to Him. Trust that He knows what you need in both.

†

OCTOBER 19

The day is Yours, the night also is Yours; You have prepared the light and the sun. You have set all the borders of the earth; You have made summer and winter. (Psalm 74:16-17)

Cultivate → Just as a tree doesn't resist the seasons, neither should we. Rather than fighting where God has placed you, embrace it with trust. If you're in a season of growth, praise Him for His provision. If you're in a season of pruning, trust that He's refining you for something greater.

Today, create a "Season List." Write down what season of life you feel you're in—whether it's one of abundance, challenge, or waiting. Then, next to it, write one way you can respond in faith. It may be serving someone else during your season of blessing or choosing to praise God even when things feel barren.

"Lord, You are the God of every season. Help me to trust Your timing and embrace where I am with gratitude and peace. Strengthen me in winter, humble me in summer, and remind me that You are always working for my good. Amen."

†

OCTOBER 20

A man's heart plans his way, but the Lord directs his steps. (Proverbs 16:9)

Contemplate → Have you ever watched a potter at the wheel? The clay spins, shaped by the potter's hands, yet the potter alone determines the final form. The clay may stretch one way, yet with just a slight press, the potter reshapes it according to his design.

Our lives are much the same. We may plan our own path—setting goals, plotting decisions, and pursuing ambitions—but God's hands are the ones shaping our journey. When He redirects us, it's not to destroy what we've envisioned but to craft something far better than we imagined.

The potter never leaves the wheel, and God never leaves us. When our plans seem to collapse or shift unexpectedly, it's not failure—it's formation. Trust the Potter's hand, even when the shaping feels uncertain.

†

OCTOBER 21

A man's heart plans his way, but the Lord directs his steps. (Proverbs 16:9)

Cultivate → Learning to trust God's redirection isn't just about surrender—it's about recognizing His fingerprints in the unexpected. Yesterday's image of the potter reminds us that God's hands are constantly shaping our path. Today, take it a step further: embrace the moments that don't go as planned as evidence of His craftsmanship.

When plans change or disruptions come, pause and ask, *"Lord, what are You shaping here?"* Instead of frustration, choose curiosity. Trust that even when the clay feels stretched, the Potter's hand is still at work.

As a practical step, intentionally write down one unexpected moment from your day and reflect on how God may be using it to form something greater in you.

"Lord, when my plans unravel, help me see Your hand at work. Teach me to trust Your design, even when I can't yet see the final shape. Amen."

†

OCTOBER 22

This is the day the Lord has made; We will rejoice and be glad in it. (Psalm 118:24)

Contemplate → This *Psalm of Thankfulness* is simple in its truth yet deeply challenging in practice. It's easy to rejoice when life is smooth, but how do we maintain joy when circumstances are difficult?

The key lies in the first phrase: *"This is the day the Lord has made."* No matter what the day holds, it is still *His*—designed with purpose, governed by His sovereignty, and filled with opportunities to trust Him. Our response is a choice: *"We will rejoice and be glad in it."* This means choosing gratitude over grumbling, faith over fear, and praise over pessimism.

Rejoicing doesn't mean ignoring pain or pretending difficulties don't exist. It means anchoring our joy in the unchanging character of God rather than the shifting conditions of life. Whatever today holds, whether trials or triumphs, rejoice—not because of the day itself, but because of the One who holds it.

†

OCTOBER 23

This is the day the Lord has made; We will rejoice and be glad in it. (Psalm 118:24)

Cultivate → Each morning this week, before looking at your phone, before thinking about your schedule, and before allowing stress to creep in, begin your day with this declaration:

"Lord, this is Your day. No matter what comes, I choose to rejoice and be glad in it."

Then, as the day unfolds, train your heart to *find the good*. When a challenge arises, pause and ask, *"Where can I see God's hand in this?"* If you feel frustration creeping in, stop and name three things you are thankful for in that moment. If you encounter a difficult person, shift your focus to how God might be using the interaction to grow you in grace. By consistently seeking joy in the midst of trials, you cultivate a spirit of gratitude that transforms not just your days but your entire perspective.

Joy is not just an emotion—it's a discipline that strengthens your faith and deepens your trust in God's sovereignty.

†

OCTOBER 24

*** As a ring of gold in a swine's snout, so is a lovely woman who lacks discretion. (Proverbs 11:22)***

Contemplate → Discretion is the bridge between knowledge and wisdom—it's the ability to apply what is right with discernment and care. This Proverb paints a striking picture: outward beauty, no matter how valuable, is meaningless without inner character. A gold ring may be precious, but when placed in a pig's snout, it loses its worth, just as a person lacking discretion cheapens their own influence.

This wisdom extends beyond just physical beauty—it applies to how we conduct ourselves, the company we keep, and the choices we make. Without discretion, we risk attaching ourselves to things that diminish our value in Christ. The world elevates image over integrity, but Scripture calls us to a higher standard.

When we seek God's wisdom, our beauty—both inward and outward—is refined, reflecting His grace in all we do.

†

OCTOBER 25

As a ring of gold in a swine's snout, so is a lovely woman who lacks discretion. (Proverbs 11:22)

Cultivate → True discretion begins with intentionality. This week, focus on exercising sound judgment in your speech, choices, and interactions. Before making a decision, pause and ask: *Does this align with wisdom? Does this honor God?* If not, choose differently. Evaluate the voices and influences shaping your heart—if something compromises your discernment, take steps to replace it with God's truth.

Practice discretion in conversations by choosing words that uplift rather than stir division. In your actions, demonstrate wisdom by being intentional with your time and commitments. Let your character be marked by discernment, reflecting God's grace in every area of life. A life shaped by discretion is one that glorifies Him and stands apart from the fleeting values of the world.

"Lord, help me to walk in wisdom and guard my heart with discretion. Let my words, choices, and relationships reflect Your truth. Teach me to value character over appearance, so my life may bring honor to You. Amen."

✝

OCTOBER 26

Do not remember the sins of my youth, nor my transgressions; According to Your mercy remember me, for Your goodness sake, O Lord. (Psalm 25:7)

Contemplate → God's mercy rewrites our story. In this Psalm, David pleads for the Lord to forget his past failures and instead, remember him according to divine mercy. How comforting it is to know that God does not define us by our worst moments! Instead of holding our past against us, He looks at us through the lens of His grace.

The weight of our youthful sins or past transgressions can often leave us feeling unworthy. Yet, Scripture reminds us that through Christ, our past is not our identity. *"As far as the east is from the west, so far has He removed our transgressions from us"* (Psalm 103:12). God's mercy doesn't just cover our sin—it cleanses and transforms.

When we come to Him in repentance, we receive not just forgiveness but a new beginning. He remembers us for His goodness' sake, not for our failures.

†

OCTOBER 27

Do not remember the sins of my youth, nor my transgressions; According to Your mercy remember me, for Your goodness sake, O Lord. (Psalm 25:7)

Cultivate → Renewal in Christ is more than just leaving the past behind—it's walking forward in the confidence of His grace. This week, practice embracing God's forgiveness by releasing the guilt of past mistakes. Whenever a past failure comes to mind, replace it with the truth of 2 Corinthians 5:17: *"If anyone is in Christ, he is a new creation; old things have passed away, behold, all things have become new."*

Let this truth shape your mindset and actions. Choose to walk in freedom rather than shame, and extend the same mercy to others that God has extended to you. If you're holding onto something that still weighs heavy on your heart, bring it before the Lord in prayer and truly let it go.

"Lord, I trust in Your mercy to cleanse my past and renew my heart. Help me walk in the freedom of Your grace, leaving behind what You have already forgiven. Thank You for remembering me according to Your goodness and not my mistakes. Amen."

†

OCTOBER 28

As in water face reflects face, so a man's heart reveals the man. (Proverbs 27:19)

Contemplate → Just as water gives an honest reflection, the heart reveals the truth of who we are. No matter how much we try to control outward appearances, our character is ultimately shaped by what we cultivate within.

A man's heart is like a mirror, showing the true nature of his soul. It is easy to deceive ourselves with surface-level reflections, focusing on external presentation rather than internal transformation. But Scripture reminds us that *"the Lord does not see as man sees; for man looks at the outward appearance, but the Lord looks at the heart"* (1 Samuel 16:7). This means that no matter how well we disguise ourselves to others, our hearts remain transparent before God.

The question is: *What does your heart reveal? Does it reflect Christ, showing love, humility, and truth? Or does it expose pride, bitterness, or fear?* Just as we stand before a mirror to check our appearance, we must regularly stand before God's Word, allowing it to reveal our hearts and refine our character in Him.

†

OCTOBER 29

As in water face reflects face, so a man's heart reveals the man. (Proverbs 27:19)

Cultivate → Begin the habit of a spiritual heart check by taking a few moments each evening to reflect on your thoughts, words, and actions from the day. *Were they aligned with God's truth, or did they reveal areas that need refining?* Ask the Holy Spirit to highlight anything that needs to be surrendered, cleansed, or redirected in your heart.

As you cultivate this habit, let God's Word be the mirror that guides you. Memorize and meditate on Psalm 139:23-24: *"Search me, O God, and know my heart; Try me, and know my anxieties; And see if there is any wicked way in me, And lead me in the way everlasting."*

"Lord, I desire a heart that reflects You. Show me where I need to grow, and shape my character according to Your truth. Help me to live with integrity, so that what is seen in my heart is pleasing in Your sight. Amen."

†

OCTOBER 30

The words of the Lord are pure words, like silver tried in a furnace of earth, purified seven times.
(Psalm 12:6)

Contemplate → Words have power. They can build up or tear down, heal or wound, guide or mislead. But unlike human speech, which can be flawed or manipulative, God's words are pure, perfect, and tested.

When silver is refined in fire, impurities burn away, leaving only what is valuable. The Psalmist uses this image to illustrate how God's words are unwavering in truth—refined to perfection.

The world bombards us with opinions, deception, and shifting narratives, but God's Word remains a secure foundation. His Word refines our thoughts, burns away lies, and shapes us in truth.

This time of year, many are drawn to themes of darkness and illusion, but God's Word shines as a light, exposing lies and bringing clarity. While some celebrate the eerie and unknown, we are called to dwell on what is true, noble, and pure (Philippians 4:8). Instead of being entertained by what unsettles, focus on the words that bring life, peace, and truth.

†

OCTOBER 31

The words of the Lord are pure words, like silver tried in a furnace of earth, purified seven times.
(Psalm 12:6)

Cultivate → The world thrives on the mysterious and misleading, but as believers, we hold to what is pure and true. Challenge yourself today to fill your mind with God's words rather than the world's distractions.

Choose a verse that counters deception or fear—perhaps Psalm 119:105 *("Your word is a lamp to my feet and a light to my path")*—and commit it to memory. Repeat it throughout the day, letting its truth refine your thoughts and shape your responses.

As darkness deceives, let God's Word filter out doubt, anxiety, and confusion. When tempted to be influenced by worldly voices, recall His promises instead. His Word doesn't just expose deception—it drives it out.

"Lord, in a world filled with deception, help me cling to Your truth. Purify my thoughts and guide my heart to treasure Your words above all else. Let Your light shine in the darkness, and may I reflect Your truth in all I say and do. Amen."

†

NOVEMBER 1

Hatred stirs up strife, but love covers all sins.
(Proverbs 10:12)

Contemplate → Firefighters know that some fires can't be extinguished by water alone—instead, they must be smothered. Depriving the flames of oxygen stops them from spreading. Hatred acts like a raging fire, consuming relationships, stirring strife, and feeding off bitterness. But love? Love is the blanket that smothers the flames before they rage out of control.

"Love covers all sins" doesn't mean love ignores sin—it means love refuses to fuel it. Jesus's sacrifice was the ultimate covering—He didn't overlook sin; He paid for it. His love smothered the flames of wrath with overwhelming mercy.

When we love someone despite their flaws, we mirror His grace. Love doesn't erase sin, but it refuses to give it power to destroy. Instead of fanning the flames of conflict, choose to cover offenses with Christ's love—a love that heals, protects, and restores.

†

NOVEMBER 2

Hatred stirs up strife, but love covers all sins.
(Proverbs 10:12)

Cultivate → Just as firefighters smother flames to stop a fire, you have the power to extinguish strife with love. This week, identify a situation where bitterness or tension has been building—whether at home, work, or within a relationship. Instead of feeding the fire, choose to cover it with love.

This may mean offering a kind word where anger was expected, sending an encouraging note, or choosing to pray for someone who has hurt you. Love may not erase the pain instantly, but it will smother the enemy's attempt to turn hurt into hatred.

"Lord, just as You covered me with Your mercy, teach me to cover others with grace. Let my love be an active force that brings peace where strife once raged. Amen."

†

NOVEMBER 3

Let us come before His presence with thanksgiving; Let us shout joyfully to Him with psalms. (Psalm 95:2)

Contemplate → Gratitude is like a key that unlocks the door to God's presence. Imagine standing outside a home filled with warmth, light, and joy—but instead of stepping in, you linger outside, weighed down by complaints or worries. Thanksgiving is the key that invites you inside.

The Hebrew word for thanksgiving here is *todah*, meaning a confession of praise—sometimes offered *before* the blessing arrives. It's choosing to trust that God is working even when circumstances seem uncertain. This kind of praise isn't just reactionary; it's prophetic. It declares that God is good *before* you see the outcome.

The Greek word for worship, *proskuneo*, means "to turn and kiss." True worship isn't distant—it's a close embrace, an expression of love and trust. When gratitude fills our hearts, we draw nearer to God, knowing He is both faithful in the past and present in our future. Gratitude doesn't just change our mood—it changes our mindset, aligning us with the presence of the One who deserves our thanks.

†

NOVEMBER 4

Let us come before His presence with thanksgiving; Let us shout joyfully to Him with psalms. (Psalm 95:2)

Cultivate → Gratitude doesn't happen by accident—it's cultivated through practice. This week, create a "Gratitude Journal" to intentionally record your blessings. Each morning, write down one thing you're thankful for—even if it's as simple as a restful night or the gift of breath.

Then, before bed, write down one way you *saw* God's goodness during the day. Whether in a conversation, a provision, or a moment of peace, this reflection will train your heart to notice His presence.

Finally, challenge yourself to speak or sing a psalm of thanksgiving—even if you're facing hardship. Gratitude is not dependent on perfect circumstances; it's anchored in the perfect character of God.

"Lord, I choose gratitude as my posture of worship. Open my eyes to see Your goodness in every moment, and let my thanksgiving draw me closer to You. Amen."

†

NOVEMBER 5

A man's steps are of the Lord; How then can a man understand his own way? (Proverbs 20:24)

Contemplate → Life often feels like navigating through fog—uncertain, unclear, and unpredictable. Imagine driving on a winding road at night. Your headlights don't reveal the entire journey—they only illuminate a few feet ahead. Yet that small circle of light is enough to keep you moving forward.

God's guidance often works the same way. He may not reveal the full picture, but He gives just enough clarity for the next step. Trying to force answers or predict the entire journey can lead to frustration, but trusting God allows you to move forward with confidence, even when you can't see what's ahead.

His peace surpasses understanding because we're not called to figure everything out—we're called to follow the One who already knows the way (Philippians 4:7). Trust that each step He orders is intentional, even when the road ahead seems unclear.

†

NOVEMBER 6

A man's steps are of the Lord; How then can a man understand his own way? (Proverbs 20:24)

Cultivate → Just as God is guiding your steps, He may use *you* to guide someone else. This week, be intentional about reaching out to someone who feels lost or uncertain. Perhaps they're facing a difficult decision, a season of waiting, or an unexpected detour.

Share a word of encouragement, a personal testimony, or a verse like Proverbs 20:24 to remind them that God is still leading—even when the path feels unclear. As you encourage others, ask God to deepen your own trust in His timing and direction.

"Lord, thank You for directing my steps, even when I don't understand the path ahead. Help me rest in Your wisdom and offer encouragement to those who feel uncertain. Remind us that Your ways are always good, and that trusting You is far greater than understanding everything. Amen."

†

NOVEMBER 7

You are my portion, O Lord; I have said that I would keep Your words. (Psalm 119:57)

Contemplate → In ancient times, inheritance was everything. Land, wealth, and status were passed down, and a person's portion defined their security and future. Yet, the psalmist declares something far greater— *"You are my portion, O Lord."* Instead of seeking earthly gain, he claimed God Himself as his inheritance.

This was more than just poetic language—it was a bold statement of trust. To call God our portion is to say, *"No matter what I lose, I still have enough."* When life feels unfair or when others seem to have more, this truth grounds us: If we have God, we have the greatest treasure of all.

We may not always see it in the moment, but in time, we'll realize that no earthly possession compares to the presence, peace, and promises we've been given in Christ.

†

NOVEMBER 8

You are my portion, O Lord; I have said that I would keep Your words. (Psalm 119:57)

Cultivate → True contentment begins when we focus on what we already have rather than what we feel is missing. This week, whenever you catch yourself feeling discontent or frustrated, pause and intentionally thank God for one way He's been enough for you.

As a practical step, write down five spiritual riches you have in Christ—His grace, His presence, His promises, His forgiveness, His guidance—and post that list where you'll see it daily. Let it remind you that no matter what the world says you lack, in Him you have everything you need.

"Lord, thank You for being my portion and my provider. Help me to trust in Your sufficiency, knowing that Your presence is greater than any earthly gain. Teach me to find contentment in You alone. Amen."

†

NOVEMBER 9

For a righteous man may fall seven times and rise again, but the wicked shall fall by calamity.
(Proverbs 24:16)

Contemplate → In Japanese culture, there's a proverb that says, *"Fall seven times, stand up eight."* It's a phrase often used in martial arts, but it reflects a profound spiritual truth—resilience isn't about avoiding failure but refusing to stay down.

The righteous are not immune to hardship; they stumble, just like everyone else. But their strength comes from knowing they don't rise alone. God's grace steadies their feet and lifts their head. Meanwhile, the wicked fall by calamity because they rely on themselves—and when they're knocked down, they have nothing greater to lean on.

If you've felt defeated lately, remember that God is the One reaching down to pull you back up. Rising isn't about your strength—it's about His. So, fall seven times if you must … just be sure to rise again.

†

NOVEMBER 10

For a righteous man may fall seven times and rise again, but the wicked shall fall by calamity.
(Proverbs 24:16)

Cultivate → Spiritual resilience is built one choice at a time. This week, identify one area where you've struggled to "rise again." Whether it's a lingering failure, discouragement, or spiritual setback, take one step forward. It could be reaching out for accountability, resuming a habit of prayer or Bible reading, or simply confessing your struggle to God in honesty.

Then, write down this truth somewhere visible: *"Falling is not final; rising is a choice."* Let it remind you that each new step forward is a victory in itself.

"Lord, when I stumble, lift me by Your strength. Help me rise again—not by my own willpower, but by trusting in Your grace. Strengthen my heart so I may press on, knowing that in You, every fall can become a testimony of Your faithfulness. Amen."

†

NOVEMBER 11

The steps of a good man are ordered by the Lord, and He delights in his way. Though he fall, he shall not be utterly cast down; for the Lord upholds him with His hand. (Psalm 37:23-24)

Contemplate → Have you ever watched a parent teaching their child to walk? The child stumbles, wobbles, and often falls. But each time, the parent is right there—arms outstretched—ready to catch, steady, or comfort. The child's steps aren't perfect, but they are guided.

That's the picture this Psalm paints. Our steps are *"ordered"* by God—not controlled like a puppet on strings, but lovingly guided like a father helping his child take each step forward. And when we stumble (because we will), His hand is there—not to condemn, but to catch us.

Peter's stumble on the water wasn't the end of his story, and your stumbles aren't the end of yours either (Matthew 14:30-31). His hand is always there to steady you. The key isn't walking flawlessly—it's trusting the One who's walking beside you.

†

NOVEMBER 12

The steps of a good man are ordered by the Lord, and He delights in his way. Though he fall, he shall not be utterly cast down; for the Lord upholds him with His hand. (Psalm 37:23-24)

Cultivate → Just as a child learns to trust their parent's hand, we must train our hearts to trust God's. Each morning this week, before stepping out the door, pause and pray:

"Lord, I trust You to guide my steps today. No matter what happens, I believe You are with me, ready to uphold me when I stumble."

Then, practice walking in that trust. If anxiety creeps in or frustration rises, stop and silently repeat that prayer. Let it redirect your heart to the One who's guiding you, step by step.

"Father, thank You for delighting in my steps—even the imperfect ones. Help me trust Your hand to uphold me, and teach me to walk with confidence in Your guidance. Amen."

†

NOVEMBER 13

A friend loves at all times, and a brother is born for adversity. (Proverbs 17:17)

Contemplate → History tells the story of Ernest Shackleton's Antarctic expedition—a journey marked by hardship and survival. After his ship, *Endurance*, was crushed by ice, Shackleton and his crew faced months of brutal conditions. Yet despite hunger, cold, and uncertainty, Shackleton's loyalty to his men never wavered. He risked his life time and again to ensure every man returned home safely.

True friendship mirrors that same spirit—showing up when others are stranded in life's icy storms. Proverbs reminds us that while anyone can celebrate with you in good times, a true friend steps into the cold and refuses to leave your side. Who has been that kind of friend in your life? And who might need you to be that person right now?

Love that endures at all times is the truest reflection of Christ's love in us.

†

NOVEMBER 14

A friend loves at all times, and a brother is born for adversity. (Proverbs 17:17)

Cultivate → As we read yesterday, just as Shackleton fought for his crew's survival, we are called to stand firm for those enduring adversity. This week, become that steady presence for someone in need. Offer your support through a practical act of love—whether by providing a meal, sitting in silence with someone who's grieving, or simply being present without expecting anything in return.

If you've been blessed by a loyal friend, take time to express gratitude. Write a note, send a message, or speak face-to-face, letting them know their presence in your life has made a difference. Relationships deepen when we choose to invest in them.

"Lord, thank You for the friends who have stood by me in difficult times. Help me be that kind of friend to others—faithful, present, and unwavering. Show me where I am needed most, and give me the courage to show up in love. Amen."

†

NOVEMBER 15

For You will light my lamp; The Lord my God will enlighten my darkness. For by You I can run against a troop, by my God I can leap over a wall. As for God, His way is perfect; the word of the Lord is proven; He is a shield to all who trust in Him
(Psalm 18:28-30)

Contemplate → Darkness distorts reality. In a pitch-black room, shadows stretch farther than they should, and objects appear larger or more threatening than they really are. Fear thrives in the unknown. But when light breaks in, clarity replaces confusion.

David declares that God doesn't just bring light—He *is* the light. His presence pierces the uncertainty that tries to overwhelm us. When we trust Him, He reveals the path forward, exposing false fears and illuminating the way. David's words remind us that God's light doesn't merely reveal a path of survival—it reveals a path of strength. With His guidance, we aren't left cowering in the dark; *but by our God, we can run against a troop and we can leap over a wall.*

God's Word has already proven true, and His presence is our steady light. No matter how overwhelming the darkness seems, it can never overpower the One who lights your way.

†

NOVEMBER 16

For You will light my lamp; The Lord my God will enlighten my darkness. For by You I can run against a troop, by my God I can leap over a wall. As for God, His way is perfect; the word of the Lord is proven; He is a shield to all who trust in Him.
(Psalm 18:28-30)

Cultivate → God's light shines brightest when we step forward in trust. This week, identify one "wall" in your life—a fear, a challenge, or a doubt that's been keeping you stuck.

Write it down as a symbol of the obstacle you're facing. Then, beneath it, write this truth: *"By my God, I can leap over a wall."* Commit to taking one bold step of faith—whether that's starting a difficult conversation, stepping into a new opportunity, or releasing control over something you've been trying to handle alone. Trust that as you move forward, God will provide the light, strength, and shield you need.

"Lord, when darkness surrounds me, help me to trust in Your light. Teach me to take bold steps of faith, knowing that Your proven Word will never fail me. I trust You to lead me over every obstacle and through every challenge. Amen."

†

NOVEMBER 17

The way of life winds upward for the wise, that he may turn away from hell below. (Proverbs 15:24)

Contemplate → Climbing a mountain requires more than strength—it demands focus. Trail markers guide the way, yet one careless step can lead to a dangerous slip. The higher you ascend, the narrower the path becomes, requiring greater attention to every step.

In this Proverb, the "way of life" is like that mountain climb—winding, challenging, and steep. It demands wisdom, endurance, and trust in God's direction. The journey isn't easy, but every step upward draws you closer to God and farther from the dangers below.

Jesus is the ultimate trail guide—His wisdom marks the path that leads to life. When we follow Him, we climb higher, leaving behind the pitfalls that drag others downward. The wise fix their eyes on Him, knowing that even when the path is difficult, He is leading them home.

†

NOVEMBER 18

The way of life winds upward for the wise, that he may turn away from hell below. (Proverbs 15:24)

Cultivate → When following Jesus, every choice moves us either upward or downward—there is no neutral ground. This week, take inventory of your daily habits and ask: Are my actions leading me toward Christ, or pulling me away?

Choose one specific habit to adjust or remove if it's pulling you in the wrong direction, and replace it with something that strengthens your walk with Christ. Whether it's setting aside more time for prayer, reducing distractions, or deepening your study of God's Word, take intentional steps to keep your path winding *upward.*

"Lord, I desire to walk in Your way, the only path to life. Reveal anything that hinders my upward journey and help me to choose wisdom daily. Strengthen me as I follow You, knowing that every step with You leads to truth, purpose, and eternal life. Amen."

†

NOVEMBER 19

For He satisfies the longing soul and fills the hungry soul with goodness. (Psalm 107:9)

Contemplate → There's a hunger within us that no meal, achievement, or relationship can fully satisfy. It's the kind of emptiness that can leave us restless, even when life seems full. History shows this truth in unexpected places. Famous figures who seemed to "have it all" often confessed to feeling unfulfilled—proof that the soul's deepest craving isn't satisfied by status or success.

In Psalm 107, the psalmist points to the true answer: God alone satisfies the longing soul. Jesus revealed this truth when He multiplied the loaves and fish, meeting a crowd's physical hunger while pointing to something greater—their need for Him. The bread filled their stomachs, but His presence was what truly nourished their souls.

If you've felt restless, empty, or unsatisfied, know this: that longing is a divine invitation. It's God calling you closer, ready to fill you with the goodness that only He provides.

†

NOVEMBER 20

For He satisfies the longing soul and fills the hungry soul with goodness. (Psalm 107:9)

Cultivate → Hunger is natural, but what you feed your soul with determines your spiritual health. This week, practice "soul fasting"—not by avoiding food, but by replacing empty distractions with meaningful moments of connection with God.

For example, when you feel the urge to scroll through your phone, pause instead for a moment of prayer or to read a verse of Scripture. When you're tempted to reach for something to "fill the void"—whether it's social media, entertainment, or even busyness—redirect that longing toward God.

As you intentionally choose Him over distractions, you'll discover that His presence satisfies in a way nothing else can.

"Lord, when my soul feels restless, help me turn to You instead of empty pursuits. Satisfy me with Your goodness and teach me to hunger for what truly fulfills. Amen."

†

NOVEMBER 21

As far as the east is from the west, so far has He removed our transgressions from us. (Psalm 103:12)

Contemplate → Some things are hard to comprehend—like the concept of infinity. The distance *"east from west"* isn't just far; it's immeasurable. Unlike north and south, which meet at the poles, east and west never intersect. They continue indefinitely in opposite directions. That's the distance God has placed between you and your sins—a distance that cannot be measured or undone.

The enemy will try to convince you otherwise. He will whisper reminders of past failures, urging you to carry a burden God has already cast away. But the truth of this verse silences those lies: when God forgives, He removes. Your sins are not misplaced—they are gone.

The next time guilt attempts to weigh you down, remember that your past has been flung so far from you that it can never return. God's mercy has drawn the ultimate line—a distance no regret can cross because of the cross.

†

NOVEMBER 22

As far as the east is from the west, so far has He removed our transgressions from us. (Psalm 103:12)

Cultivate → Freedom flourishes when we extend grace to others as freely as we've received it. Today, identify one person you've struggled to forgive—whether it's someone from your past or someone you're currently at odds with. Pray specifically for their well-being today, asking God to soften your heart and fill you with His mercy.

As you pray, reflect on how God has removed your sins. Let that truth fuel your decision to release bitterness or resentment. Forgiveness isn't always immediate, but each prayer is a step closer to walking in the freedom Christ has already given you.

"Lord, thank You for removing my sins as far as the east is from the west. As You have forgiven me, help me to forgive others. Soften my heart, heal my wounds, and free me from the weight of bitterness. Amen."

†

NOVEMBER 23

My soul melts from heaviness; Strengthen me according to Your word. (Psalm 119:28)

Contemplate → There's a reason the phrase "melting under pressure" is so familiar—it captures what happens when life's burdens seem to dissolve our resolve. Stress, grief, or discouragement can feel like a weight pressing us down, leaving us powerless to stand. The psalmist knew this feeling well, describing his soul as melting under the strain.

But notice his response—he doesn't rely on inner strength or human solutions. He turns to God's Word as the antidote to his exhaustion. Scripture isn't just comforting; it's stabilizing. It restores what's crumbling inside us, reinforcing our spirit when we feel we're sinking.

Just as metal must melt before it can be reforged, sometimes God allows the pressure to soften what needs reshaping. He doesn't let us melt to destroy us—but to remold us into something stronger. When heaviness threatens to overwhelm you, lean on the promises of God. His Word doesn't merely inspire—it anchors you in truth, stabilizing what feels like it's slipping away. Strength comes not from striving harder but from standing firmer on His unshakable Word.

†

NOVEMBER 24

My soul melts from heaviness; Strengthen me according to Your word. (Psalm 119:28)

Cultivate → When your soul feels heavy, take a moment today to physically open your Bible and read a passage of God's Word aloud. Let His truth fill the air around you and settle in your heart.

There is power in hearing the very words that have the strength to lift and restore us. Even if it's just a single verse, speaking Scripture out loud reminds us that God's promises are alive and active. When heaviness weighs on you, let His Word be the foundation that upholds you.

"Lord, when my soul melts from heaviness, I choose to stand on Your Word. Let it strengthen me, renew my mind, and bring peace to my heart. Thank You for being my refuge and restoring my spirit through Your truth. Amen."

†

Matthew Maher

NOTHING NEW UNDER THE SUN

Matthew Maher

"Nothing new under the sun."

This familiar phrase speaks to the reality of life in our fallen world—a world marked by repetition, cycles, and fleeting pursuits. King Solomon, the son of David and widely regarded as the wisest man to walk this earth—besides Christ Himself—used this profound statement as the foundation for his reflections in Ecclesiastes.

With remarkable wisdom, Solomon explores the frustrations and fleeting nature of life "under the sun." Yet in doing so, he points to a greater truth—a way to live with purpose, joy, and eternal significance even in a world that is passing away.

In this final section, I've chosen select verses from Ecclesiastes that are often overlooked yet rich with insight—timeless lessons that echo the wisdom found in Psalms and Proverbs. Though brief, these verses pour out deep truths like fine wine, revealing the *ProPs* needed to live with heavenly focus while still grounded in earthly realities.

Here's the key: The man who lives for the Son while walking under the sun will be made new—even in a world that remains old.

Embrace the SUPPORT!

NOVEMBER 25

That which has been is what will be, that which is done is what will be done, and there is nothing new under the sun. (Ecclesiastes 1:9)

Contemplate → History has a way of repeating itself. Trends resurface, ideologies recycle, and human struggles remain remarkably familiar. It's like walking in circles—same patterns, just with a different face. What feels "new" often reveals itself as yesterday's rebellion repackaged in today's culture.

But while the world spins on this endless loop, Christ offers something altogether different—newness. In Him, the cycles of sin and despair are broken. Old regrets lose their grip. Chains that bound generations before are shattered by His transforming power. The world may keep repeating itself, but the heart surrendered to Christ walks in freedom—no longer trapped by the patterns of the past.

You may have seen this world's ways before, but are you embracing the new life Christ offers you today?

†

NOVEMBER 26

That which has been is what will be, that which is done is what will be done, and there is nothing new under the sun. (Ecclesiastes 1:9)

Cultivate → While the world spins in cycles, God's mercies break the loop. Today, ask God to reveal one area of your life where you've been stuck in repetition—whether it's negativity, doubt, or unhealthy habits. Choose one intentional step toward renewal: replace anxious thoughts with words of faith, turn your focus from comparison to contentment, or break the cycle of self-reliance by committing to deeper prayer.

Let your response be a reflection of Christ's transforming power—a small yet significant step toward something new under the Son.

"Lord, thank You for the newness You bring each day. Show me where I've been stuck in unhealthy cycles, and lead me in Your path of renewal. Help me walk in Your freedom today. Amen."

†

NOVEMBER 27

For in much wisdom is much grief, and he who increases knowledge increases sorrow.
(Ecclesiastes 1:18)

Contemplate → Gaining wisdom can feel like putting on a new pair of glasses—suddenly, you see things more clearly, but not everything you see is pleasant. Hidden flaws, brokenness, and the reality of sin come into sharper focus. The more you understand, the heavier the burden can feel.

Jesus, the embodiment of perfect wisdom, carried this burden. He wept over Jerusalem, grieved the hardness of people's hearts, and mourned the weight of sin (Luke 19:41). Yet He didn't allow sorrow to silence His purpose—He moved forward in love, healing, and hope.

Wisdom's grief is not meant to crush us but to cultivate compassion. When we entrust that burden to Christ, we find the strength to walk in understanding without being overwhelmed by it. His wisdom reveals the world's brokenness, but it also reveals His power to restore it.

†

NOVEMBER 28

For in much wisdom is much grief, and he who increases knowledge increases sorrow.
(Ecclesiastes 1:18)

Cultivate → True wisdom should not paralyze us with grief but propel us toward godly action. Instead of dwelling on the weight of what you know, let it shape how you respond. Today, choose one way to act on your wisdom—whether it's speaking truth in love, comforting someone struggling with hardship, or praying for God's guidance in an area where you feel burdened.

Wisdom is not meant to be carried alone but entrusted to God, who strengthens us to walk in it.

"Lord, as I grow in wisdom, help me to trust You with the sorrow that comes with it. Let my understanding lead to compassion, not despair. Show me how to use the knowledge You've given me to serve, love, and act according to Your will. Amen."

†

NOVEMBER 29

Then the dust will return to the earth as it was, and the spirit will return to God who gave it.
(Ecclesiastes 12:7)

Contemplate → Picture an hourglass—grains of sand steadily falling, each grain marking a passing moment. No one can stop the flow; time continues until the final grain drops. This verse reminds us that our bodies are like that dust—fragile and finite—while our spirits are eternal, returning to the God who breathed life into us.

But while our days may seem to slip away like sand through our fingers, God calls us to live each one with purpose. For those who trust in Christ, the end is not an empty void but a divine homecoming. Just as the hourglass must be turned to begin again, our earthly lives give way to a new and eternal beginning in His presence.

The question is not whether our lives will run out of time—it's how we will use the moments we've been given. Are you investing in what will outlast this life, or are you consumed by things that will crumble like dust?

†

NOVEMBER 30

__Then the dust will return to the earth as it was, and the spirit will return to God who gave it.__
__(Ecclesiastes 12:7)__

Cultivate → Life is a brief breath, and every day we draw closer to the moment when our spirit returns to its Maker. Instead of fearing death, live with eternal purpose today. Take time to reflect on one way you can prepare for eternity—whether by deepening your relationship with Christ, making amends with someone, or investing in what truly matters.

Many avoid thinking about death, yet Scripture calls us to number our days so that we may gain wisdom (Psalm 90:12). If today were your last, what legacy would you leave behind? What spiritual impact are you making? Rather than pushing these thoughts aside, let them shape the way you live. Speak words of life, extend love to others, and set your priorities on things that last beyond this world.

Lord, remind me daily that my life is a gift, not to be wasted on fleeting pursuits but to be lived in light of eternity. Help me prepare my heart for the day I return to You. Amen.

†

DECEMBER 1

As you do not know what is the way of the wind, or how the bones grow in the womb of her who is with child, so you do not know the works of God who makes everything. (Ecclesiastes 11:5)

Contemplate → Life is filled with moments that leave us searching for answers—unexpected loss, unanswered prayers, or closed doors we thought were meant to open. In those times, it's easy to wonder, *What is God doing?* Yet this verse reminds us that God's work is often hidden from our understanding.

Just as the wind follows a path we cannot trace, so God's hand moves in ways we cannot predict. And just as a baby develops in the womb—unseen yet unmistakably formed—so too does God's purpose unfold in His perfect timing. We may not always understand the "how" or the "why," but we can trust the One who knows all things and holds our lives in His hands.

When you can't see what God is doing, will you trust that He is working in the unseen?

†

DECEMBER 2

As you do not know what is the way of the wind, or how the bones grow in the womb of her who is with child, so you do not know the works of God who makes everything. (Ecclesiastes 11:5)

Cultivate → When God's work seems hidden, it's tempting to focus on what we *don't* see. Instead, shift your focus to what you *do* know—His faithfulness.

Today, recall a time when you couldn't see what God was doing until later. Use this memory as a reminder of His unseen hand guiding you. Then, share that testimony with someone who's currently struggling to trust God's plan. Your words may become the encouragement they need to trust Him in their own season of uncertainty.

"Lord, when I can't see what You're doing, I choose to remember what You've already done. Thank You for working in the unseen, guiding my life with wisdom and love. Help me to encourage others to trust You in their waiting. Amen."

†

DECEMBER 3

Then I saw that wisdom excels folly as light excels darkness. The wise man's eyes are in his head, but the fool walks in darkness. Yet I myself perceived that the same event happens to them all. (Ecclesiastes 2:13-14)

Contemplate → Wisdom is like having a map in unfamiliar territory. Think about two travelers hiking a mountain trail—one equipped with a detailed map and compass, the other guessing his way forward. The one with the map may still face unexpected obstacles, but he knows how to adjust his steps and stay on course. The one without guidance is left wandering, vulnerable to pitfalls and wrong turns.

This is the difference between wisdom and folly. Wisdom doesn't remove life's challenges, but it equips us to navigate them with clarity and purpose. Meanwhile, folly leaves us unprepared, relying on guesswork in a world filled with uncertainty.

Yet, Solomon points out a sobering truth—both travelers face the same reality: life's end. The difference is that wisdom prepares us for what's beyond the trail. When we follow Christ, wisdom doesn't just guide us through this life—it leads us safely home.

†

DECEMBER 4

Then I saw that wisdom excels folly as light excels darkness. The wise man's eyes are in his head, but the fool walks in darkness. Yet I myself perceived that the same event happens to them all. (Ecclesiastes 2:13-14)

Cultivate → Wisdom isn't just about avoiding bad choices—it's about embracing God's direction even when it doesn't make sense.

This week, practice listening for God's wisdom in unexpected places. Pay attention to a sermon, a conversation, or a verse that seems to challenge your thinking. Rather than brushing it aside, ask God to show you how His wisdom applies to your situation.

Then take one deliberate step of obedience—whether that means adjusting your attitude, seeking forgiveness, or stepping out in faith when you'd rather stay comfortable. Wisdom isn't just knowing what's right—it's choosing to act on it.

"Lord, give me ears to hear Your wisdom and a heart willing to follow it. When Your truth confronts my comfort or pride, help me surrender and walk in obedience. Lead me in the path that honors You. Amen."

†

DECEMBER 5

He who digs a pit will fall into it, and whoever breaks through a wall will be bitten by a serpent.
(Ecclesiastes 10:8)

Contemplate → In ancient times, farmers would sometimes dig hidden pits to trap wild animals. The irony was that careless digging or poor placement could lead to the trapper falling into his own pit. In the same way, the walls they built weren't just property markers—they protected homes, livestock, and crops from danger. Breaking through such a wall wasn't just careless—it invited risk.

This verse reminds us that our choices create outcomes. Digging pits—whether through dishonesty, pride, or sinful habits—often leads to self-destruction. Likewise, when we push past God's protective boundaries—ignoring His wisdom in relationships, integrity, or priorities—we expose ourselves to danger.

This truth goes back to the very beginning. In the Garden of Eden, God established a boundary for Adam and Eve—not to restrict them, but to protect them. Yet when they ignored His command and reached beyond the limit He set, they found themselves face to face with the serpent. Breaking through God's boundary unleashed consequences they couldn't contain.

Matthew Maher

The traps we set for others can turn on us, and the boundaries we break often expose us to unseen dangers. Sin may feel safe at first—like digging a shallow pit—but sooner or later, the ground gives way. The best safeguard? Walk wisely, trust God's limits, and stop digging holes where you're meant to stand firm.

†

DECEMBER 6

He who digs a pit will fall into it, and whoever breaks through a wall will be bitten by a serpent.
(Ecclesiastes 10:8)

Cultivate → If sin, bad decisions, or neglect has created a pit in your life, don't let shame keep you there. God specializes in rescuing those who call on Him.

Today, take one intentional step to address a "pit" in your life. Whether it's apologizing to someone you've wronged, breaking free from a harmful habit, or seeking accountability in an area where you've been compromising, choose to climb out rather than dig deeper.

Likewise, if you've been pressing against a boundary God has set, ask Him for the strength to turn back before regret follows. Adam and Eve's story reminds us that God's boundaries are not roadblocks—they are guardrails designed to keep us safe. Trust His wisdom, knowing that His boundaries are not to withhold good from you, but to protect you from harm.

"Lord, reveal the pits in my life and give me the courage to turn back before I fall deeper. Help me to trust the boundaries You've placed for my protection. Amen."

†

DECEMBER 7

If the ax is dull, and one does not sharpen the edge, then he must use more strength; but wisdom brings success. (Ecclesiastes 10:10)

Contemplate → Abraham Lincoln famously said, *"Give me six hours to chop down a tree, and I will spend the first four sharpening the ax."* His point? Preparation determines success. Swinging harder with a dull blade may feel productive, but it wastes energy and yields little progress.

This proverb illustrates that wisdom is the sharpening process in our lives. Without wisdom, we often attempt to power through life's challenges with brute force—reacting impulsively, relying on our own strength, or ignoring God's guidance. But when we sharpen ourselves spiritually, emotionally, and mentally, we gain clarity, precision, and endurance.

God's Word sharpens our minds with truth. Prayer sharpens our hearts with peace. And wise counsel sharpens our decisions with insight. Success isn't just about effort—it's about preparation. The dull ax demands more strength, but the sharp one makes each swing effective. Where do you need to stop striving and start sharpening?

†

DECEMBER 8

If the ax is dull, and one does not sharpen the edge, then he must use more strength; but wisdom brings success. (Ecclesiastes 10:10)

Cultivate → Yesterday's challenge asked you to examine what areas of your life need sharpening. Today, take action. Identify one practical way to sharpen your "ax"—whether it's investing more time in prayer, improving a skill you've neglected, or seeking advice from someone wiser than you.

Instead of relying on sheer effort, ask God to reveal where preparation can replace frustration. If your relationships feel strained, sharpen your patience with intentional listening. If your spiritual life feels stagnant, sharpen your focus with time in His Word. If your work feels overwhelming, sharpen your priorities by asking God for direction. Sharpening may take time, but the strength you save and the fruit you bear will be far greater than what you achieve by pushing forward with a dull blade.

"Lord, I don't want to wear myself out with empty striving. Show me where I need to pause, prepare, and sharpen my life with Your wisdom. Help me trust that success comes not by my strength, but by following Your ways. Amen."

†

DECEMBER 9

The words of a wise man's mouth are gracious, but the lips of a fool shall swallow him up. (Ecclesiastes 10:12)

Contemplate → Words are like seeds—they don't just disappear after they're spoken. Instead, they take root, growing into something that either nourishes or poisons those who hear them. A wise person's words plant grace, leaving others encouraged and uplifted. But a fool's careless words plant harm, and those destructive seeds often turn back on him, consuming his own reputation and relationships.

Proverbs 18:21 reminds us that *"Death and life are in the power of the tongue."* Our words shape atmospheres, influence hearts, and leave lasting impacts. Gracious words calm storms, mend wounds, and build trust. Harsh or reckless words ignite conflict, deepen division, and often return with consequences.

The difference between wisdom and foolishness isn't just in what we say—it's in *how* we say it. Wisdom speaks life. Foolishness spews poison. What are you planting with your words today?

†

DECEMBER 10

The words of a wise man's mouth are gracious, but the lips of a fool shall swallow him up. (Ecclesiastes 10:12)

Cultivate → Yesterday's challenge called you to reflect on your words—today's challenge invites you to act. Identify one conversation you know is coming today—whether it's a meeting, a family discussion, or a social media post—and commit to speaking words of grace in that moment.

If tension rises, pause before responding. If frustration stirs, ask God for the wisdom to reply with calmness. If someone is discouraged, be intentional about offering a word of encouragement.

Your words today have the power to either plant grace or stir strife. Choose to sow seeds of life.

"Lord, make me mindful of the words I speak today. When I'm tempted to respond carelessly, slow me down. Fill my speech with grace, wisdom, and kindness so that I may reflect Your truth and love. Amen."

†

DECEMBER 11

To everything there is a season, a time for every purpose under heaven. (Ecclesiastes 3:1)

Contemplate → Seasons are not just measured by the changing of weather—they are marked by shifts in our lives. Farmers know that planting and harvesting cannot happen in the same season. The same is true spiritually. There are seasons when God plants new purpose in our hearts, and there are seasons when He prunes away what no longer belongs. There are seasons of quiet preparation and seasons of rapid growth.

Consider the life of Joseph. He endured a season of betrayal, slavery, and imprisonment before stepping into a season of leadership and influence. What seemed like wasted years were actually years of preparation. Joseph's time in the pit and the prison prepared him for the palace.

Your current season is not wasted. Whether you're being planted or pruned, God is using this time to cultivate something within you. Trust that the same God who created the seasons of nature is faithfully working through the season of your life.

†

DECEMBER 12

A time to be born, and a time to die... A time to break down, and a time to build up... A time to weep, and a time to laugh... A time to mourn, and a time to dance... (Ecclesiastes 3:2-8)

Cultivate → Turn to the passage above and read all of the verses. Now consider how seasons require different responses. Wisdom is knowing *when* to embrace change and *how* to thrive within it. Today, identify one action that reflects your current season.

If you're in a season of waiting, practice patience by intentionally slowing down. If you're in a season of building, commit to small, consistent steps of progress. If you're in a season of healing, allow yourself space to rest without guilt.

Instead of fighting your season, ask God how He's inviting you to grow through it. Each step of obedience brings you closer to His purpose.

"Lord, help me recognize what You are teaching me in this season. Whether I am planting, growing, or waiting, give me the faith to trust Your timing and the courage to follow Your lead. Amen."

†

DECEMBER 13

Because of laziness the building decays, and through idleness of hands the house leaks. (Ecclesiastes 10:18)

Contemplate → Neglect rarely shows immediate consequences—it's slow, silent, and subtle. Think of a neglected garden. Weeds don't take over in a day, but gradually, they choke out healthy plants until what was once thriving becomes overgrown and lifeless. The same happens in our spiritual lives, relationships, and responsibilities.

A marriage isn't strained overnight; it's often the result of small moments left unaddressed. Faith doesn't weaken in a single day; it fades when we drift from prayer and God's Word. Even our character is vulnerable—integrity erodes when we overlook small compromises.

The warning in this verse is clear: neglect invites decay. If we ignore what God has entrusted to us, what once stood strong will begin to crumble. What areas in your life are quietly deteriorating? The sooner you address them, the stronger the foundation will remain.

†

DECEMBER 14

Because of laziness the building decays, and through idleness of hands the house leaks. (Ecclesiastes 10:18)

Cultivate → Restoration starts with responsibility. Ask yourself: *Where have I been neglecting what God has entrusted to me?* Identify one area—whether it's your spiritual life, your relationships, or even your personal discipline—and take one intentional step to strengthen it today.

If your spiritual life feels dry, commit to opening God's Word today—even for a few minutes. If a relationship has weakened, reach out with a word of encouragement or an apology. If your personal discipline has slipped, commit to one act of diligence today, however small.

Neglect is reversed by consistent, intentional action. Even small steps today can repair cracks that would otherwise grow into major damage.

"Lord, show me where I've neglected what You've given me. Strengthen my hands to rebuild what's broken and restore what's been left unattended. Help me to walk in diligence and faithfulness, trusting that You will strengthen what I surrender to You. Amen."

†

DECEMBER 15

Two are better than one, because they have a good reward for their labor. (Ecclesiastes 4:9)

Contemplate → Imagine a fire burning brightly—its flames strong and steady. If you pull one coal away from the others, that glowing ember quickly cools and fades. But when placed back in the fire, the coal regains its heat and strength.

The same is true for us. Isolation weakens our resolve, but fellowship reignites our faith. God designed us to thrive in relationships, where we are encouraged, challenged, and strengthened. Friendships that are grounded in Christ provide accountability when we falter and celebration when we succeed.

But the strongest bonds aren't just between two people—they're anchored by God Himself. When He becomes the third strand in a relationship, that connection is strengthened beyond what human effort can achieve. Are you fostering friendships that keep your faith burning bright?

†

DECEMBER 16

Two are better than one, because they have a good reward for their labor. (Ecclesiastes 4:9)

Cultivate → Healthy relationships require more than just presence—they need purpose. Today, intentionally invest in a friendship or partnership that encourages spiritual growth. Reach out to a friend and invite them to pray with you, read Scripture together, or simply talk about what God is doing in your lives.

If you're feeling disconnected, ask God to reveal someone in your life who may need encouragement or companionship. Whether by text, call, or conversation, take that first step in building a bond that glorifies God.

"Lord, thank You for the gift of relationships. Help me to invest in connections that draw me closer to You. May my friendships reflect Your love, strengthen my faith, and encourage others to walk in Your truth. Amen."

†

DECEMBER 17

For if they fall, one will lift up his companion. But woe to him who is alone when he falls, for he has no one to help him up. (Ecclesiastes 4:10)

Contemplate → In rock climbing, there's a crucial role called the *belayer*. This person stays firmly planted on the ground, holding the rope that secures the climber. If the climber slips, the belayer's job is to catch them, ensuring they don't fall far. Even the most skilled climbers know they're only as safe as the person holding the rope.

Life is no different. No matter how strong, experienced, or independent we may think we are, there will come a time when we slip. Without someone steadying us in faith, a small stumble can turn into a devastating fall.

God designed relationships to act like a belayer—someone who stands firm in truth, ready to steady us when we lose our footing. Are you investing in those kinds of friendships? And are you willing to be that kind of support for others?

†

DECEMBER 18

For if they fall, one will lift up his companion. But woe to him who is alone when he falls, for he has no one to help him up. (Ecclesiastes 4:10)

Cultivate → Strong friendships are built before the fall—not after. Today, take a proactive step to strengthen a relationship. Reach out to a friend not just because they're struggling, but because they may one day need you in their corner.

Schedule a coffee date, send a thoughtful text, or offer to pray for someone today. Investing in relationships now strengthens the net that God has placed around you both for the future.

"Lord, thank You for the people You've placed in my life. Help me to invest in friendships that build faith and bring strength. May I be a lifter to those around me, and may I welcome those You send to lift me. Amen."

†

DECEMBER 19

Again, if two lie down together, they will keep warm; But how can one be warm alone? (Ecclesiastes 4:11)

Contemplate → On that first Christmas night, the world was cold and dark. Bethlehem's streets were crowded, yet no room was found for the Savior's birth. But in the quiet of a stable, warmth was present—not from luxury or comfort, but from the presence of love itself. Mary and Joseph, huddled together with their newborn child, experienced the warmth that only God's presence can provide.

In the same way, God's design for our lives includes the warmth of companionship. Just as the Christ-child's arrival brought light and love into a cold and weary world, so too does the presence of godly relationships bring comfort during life's hardest seasons.

Loneliness can feel strongest during the holidays, but God's answer has always been connection—through family, friendship, and most importantly, through His Son. His love is the fire that keeps our hearts from growing cold.

†

DECEMBER 20

Again, if two lie down together, they will keep warm;
But how can one be warm alone? (Ecclesiastes 4:11)

Cultivate → While Christmas is a season of warmth for many, others feel the sting of distance, grief, or separation. This week, commit to sharing the warmth of Christ by sending a heartfelt Christmas card to someone who may be struggling. Personalize it with a meaningful Scripture or an encouraging note to remind them they are seen, loved, and not alone.

If possible, include a small gift—a candle, a warm pair of socks, or a simple treat—to tangibly reflect God's love and comfort. Just as God wrapped His love in the person of Jesus, your thoughtful gesture can wrap someone in the warmth of His presence.

"Lord, thank You for the comfort of Your love. Show me who I can bless this week with a reminder of Your presence. May my words and actions reflect the peace that came through Christ. Amen."

†

DECEMBER 21

__Though one may be overpowered by another, two can withstand him. And a threefold cord is not quickly broken. (Ecclesiastes 4:12)__

Contemplate → Think of the nativity scene—Mary and Joseph, two people united by faith, clinging to each other in the face of uncertainty. They had no control over their circumstances—forced to travel to Bethlehem, turned away from the inn, delivering their child in a stable. Yet, what held them together was not just their bond as a couple, but their shared trust in God. He was the third strand, weaving their lives into a strength that could endure hardship, fear, and even the very real threat of Herod's wrath.

In the same way, our relationships are strongest when Christ is the center. Human connections alone are valuable, but when He becomes the foundation, those bonds become fortified. A friendship, marriage, or family grounded in His love will stand firm through all of life's fiercest storms.

Are your most important relationships strengthened by the presence of Christ?

†

DECEMBER 22

Though one may be overpowered by another, two can withstand him. And a threefold cord is not quickly broken. (Ecclesiastes 4:12)

Cultivate → The Christmas season is an ideal time to invite Christ into your relationships. This week, find a way to deepen a key relationship by sharing a spiritual moment together. Whether it's reading the Christmas story with family, inviting a friend to a Christmas service, or gathering with loved ones to pray, be intentional in strengthening that bond with Christ as the main focus.

When we intentionally weave Him into our relationships, they become more than just connections—they become *cords of strength* that hold firm, no matter the storm. With Christ at the center, we don't just face the weather—we weather the weather with unwavering hope and enduring faith.

"Lord, thank You for the people You've placed in my life. Help me to invite You into my relationships so that they may be strengthened by Your presence. Be the unbreakable strand that binds us together in love and truth. Amen."

✝

DECEMBER 23

I returned and saw under the sun that—the race is not to the swift, nor the battle to the strong, nor bread to the wise, nor riches to men of understanding, but time and chance happen to them all. (Ecclesiastes 9:11)

Contemplate → The Christmas narrative itself is a perfect illustration of this truth. By human standards, the birth of the Messiah should have taken place in a palace, celebrated by kings and guarded by the powerful. Yet God's plan defied all earthly expectations. Jesus arrived in a humble stable, born to a carpenter and a young virgin from a small town. No position, wealth, or power influenced His arrival—only the sovereign plan of God.

In our own lives, we may feel that our efforts, wisdom, or strength should dictate the outcome. Yet time and again, God reminds us that He works in ways that defy human calculation. Just as He used a manger to usher in the King of Kings, He often chooses unlikely paths to fulfill His perfect plan.

Are you trusting in your strength or surrendering to His sovereignty?

†

DECEMBER 24

I returned and saw under the sun that—the race is not to the swift, nor the battle to the strong, nor bread to the wise, nor riches to men of understanding, but time and chance happen to them all. (Ecclesiastes 9:11)

Cultivate → The Christmas season is full of moments that remind us we're not in control—unexpected delays, unmet expectations, or changed plans. Instead of resisting those moments, use them as reminders to surrender to God's perfect timing.

Today, when something doesn't go according to plan—even if it's something small—pause and whisper this prayer: *"Lord, I trust You with this."* Practicing this habit in the little moments will help you release control in the bigger ones.

"Lord, thank You for being faithful even when my plans fail. Teach me to trust Your timing and purpose, believing that Your way is always better. Help me to surrender my expectations and rest in Your perfect will. Amen."

†

DECEMBER 25

A good name is better than precious ointment, and the day of death than the day of one's birth.
(Ecclesiastes 7:1)

Merry Christmas! On this holy day, take time to read both **Contemplate** and **Cultivate**—today's reflection is meant to be received as a whole: worship and response, remembrance and recommitment.

Contemplate → The birth of Jesus was marked by humility—no grand palace, no royal welcome, yet His name carried a purpose far greater than any king's title. His name, Jesus, meant "The Lord saves," and from His first breath, He was destined for the cross.

Think about the wise men who brought precious gifts to honor Him—gold, frankincense, and myrrh. These costly treasures symbolized His royalty, divinity, and sacrifice. Yet, the greatest treasure in that room wasn't the fragrant oils—it was the presence of Jesus, Himself.

The world values wealth, status, and appearances, but Scripture reminds us that a name built on righteousness and character carries far greater worth. As we reflect on Jesus's birth, let's also remember that our own legacy—our "name"—is shaped by the choices we make and the love we extend. May our lives echo the goodness of the One whose name is above all names.

†

DECEMBER 25 *(continued)*

A good name is better than precious ointment, and the day of death than the day of one's birth.
(Ecclesiastes 7:1)

Cultivate → Today, we celebrate the birth of the greatest name in history—Jesus Christ. His coming was not about power or wealth, but about humility, love, and redemption. The question we must ask ourselves is: what legacy are we leaving behind?

Take a moment to reflect on your own name. Is it associated with integrity, kindness, and faithfulness? As we remember the Savior's birth, consider one action you can take today to honor His name—whether through an act of kindness, a moment of gratitude, or sharing His love with someone in need. Let today be more than just a celebration; let it be a commitment to build a name that glorifies Him.

"Lord, on this day of celebration, I thank You for the greatest gift—Your Son, Jesus Christ. Help me to live in a way that honors His name, shaping my own legacy to reflect His love and truth. May my life be a testimony of Your grace, pointing others to the One whose name is above all names. Amen."

†

DECEMBER 26

***The end of a thing is better than its beginning; the patient in spirit is better than the proud in spirit.
(Ecclesiastes 7:8)***

Contemplate → A marathon runner doesn't celebrate at the starting line—the real victory comes at the finish. The starting gun may bring excitement, but it's the endurance through pain, exhaustion, and self-doubt that makes crossing the finish line so rewarding.

The same is true in life. New beginnings often feel full of potential, yet they're also marked by uncertainty, setbacks, and slow progress. But Scripture reminds us that the end is better than the beginning—not because the journey is easy, but because patience has allowed God to refine and strengthen us along the way.

Pride demands quick results, but patience trusts the process. Endurance isn't just about surviving the race—it's about trusting God's pace when progress feels slow. Whether you're facing an unfinished goal, a difficult season, or a dream that seems delayed, remember that God is not just writing your beginning—He's crafting an ending far better than you can imagine.

†

DECEMBER 27

The end of a thing is better than its beginning; the patient in spirit is better than the proud in spirit.
(Ecclesiastes 7:8)

Cultivate → Instead of racing into the new year with a list of resolutions, pause and reflect on what you need to finish first. Identify one lingering task, unresolved conflict, or neglected commitment that you can address.

It might be sending that message you've been putting off, closing out a project you've delayed, or making peace in a relationship that's strained. Ending this year well isn't about starting something new—it's about faithfully finishing what God has already placed before you.

"Lord, give me the wisdom to recognize what I need to finish before stepping into what's next. Help me to embrace patience, trusting that You are working all things for good—even the things I've left undone. Amen."

†

DECEMBER 28

Let us hear the conclusion of the whole matter; Fear God and keep His commandments, for this is man's all. For God will bring every work into judgment, including every secret thing, whether good or evil.
(Ecclesiastes 12:13-14)

Contemplate → Imagine standing at the end of a long journey, looking back at every choice you've made—each turn, each detour, each moment of progress or delay. Solomon's words in this verse are like a guide handing you a map before the journey even begins: *This is what matters most—fear God and obey Him.*

Success, reputation, and comfort can seem like the ultimate goals, but none of them last. Solomon, a man who experienced the pinnacle of wealth, power, and influence, concludes that life's true purpose is not found in what we achieve, but in how we honor God. Our unseen decisions, private thoughts, and unnoticed acts of obedience all matter because they are seen by the One who will one day make all things right. The wise choice is to live with eternity in view—to walk in reverence and trust, knowing that God sees every step.

†

DECEMBER 29

Let us hear the conclusion of the whole matter; Fear God and keep His commandments, for this is man's all. For God will bring every work into judgment, including every secret thing, whether good or evil.
(Ecclesiastes 12:13-14)

Cultivate → As the year winds down, take time to reflect with purpose. Don't just look back—look inward. Ask yourself: *Am I living for what matters most?*

Today, spend time in prayer, specifically inviting God to reveal where your heart has drifted from Him. Write down two things: one area where you've been faithful, and one area where you've compromised.

Then, commit to strengthening what's right and surrendering what's wrong. Before the new year begins, choose to align your focus with Solomon's conclusion: *Fear God and obey Him.*

"Lord, as I close this year, I surrender my heart fully to You. Strengthen my obedience, deepen my reverence, and shape me into someone who lives for what truly matters. Amen."

†

DECEMBER 30

In the day of prosperity be joyful, but in the day of adversity consider: Surely God has appointed the one as well as the other. (Ecclesiastes 7:14)

Contemplate → Life's seasons are rarely predictable, yet this verse reminds us that both prosperity and adversity are divinely appointed. We often celebrate success, answered prayers, and seasons of abundance as signs of God's favor—but what about hardship? Scripture calls us to *consider* adversity—to pause and reflect on what God is doing through it.

Think of the Israelites at the Red Sea. After witnessing God's miraculous deliverance from Egypt, they stood with their backs to the water, cornered by Pharaoh's army. It seemed like disaster—but God was working. That moment of adversity became the stage for one of the greatest displays of His power. The waters parted, and what seemed like an ending became a new beginning.

The same is true for you. God is just as present in the storms as He is in the sunshine. Prosperity may fill your hands, but adversity shapes your heart. As you reflect on this past year, consider how even the hard moments were part of His greater plan. The same God who allows adversity has already prepared a path through it—and He never wastes a trial.

†

DECEMBER 31

In the day of prosperity be joyful, but in the day of adversity consider: Surely God has appointed the one as well as the other. (Ecclesiastes 7:14)

Cultivate → As you prepare to step into the new year, take a moment to reflect on both the triumphs and trials of this past year. Write down one victory where you experienced God's blessing—and one adversity where you felt His refining hand.

Now, turn each into a prayer. For the victory, thank Him for His provision. For the hardship, thank Him for the strength He provided and the growth He produced in you.

Then, declare this truth: *"God, You were faithful in my victories, and You were working in my struggles. I trust that You will guide me in the year ahead, for my good and Your glory."*

End this year with gratitude—not just for what you gained, but for what God is making of you. His plans are perfect, His purpose is sure, and His presence will go before you. Step into the new year with confidence, knowing He is the God of both the sunshine and the storm—and in Him, *all things have purpose.*

†

Matthew Maher

EPILOGUE

Living effectively means doing things right, while living efficiently means doing the right thing. I like that! These two living tools, coupled together, define applied wisdom. It's not just about memorizing Scripture or skimming through it intellectually—it's about living it out. The SUPPORT offered in this devotional, from the Proverbs and Psalms to the additional gems from Ecclesiastes, provides the choice *ProPs* necessary to bring balance to an unstable world.

Out of the four books in the Core Conviction Series, this one has been the most efficient and effective in nature. How so? As I dissected each Proverb and Psalm apart, I found myself living straight what I was working through while writing this book. Simply engaging with the SUPPORT offered in each verse and binding them to my daily interactions made my impact more efficient and effective—even in this crooked place called prison.

As I broke down each verse, I saw myself in the fool and placed myself in the wise. This devotional serves as a pocket mirror, reflecting the Word of God into our lives. One look at yourself through each verse, and you'll realize how crucial the SUPPORT offered is for maintaining the proper reflection of Christ in and through our lives. None of us are perfect, but in Christ, we are perfected.

I hope and pray that you will meditate on, contemplate, and cultivate the profound truths shared in each thought. Always remember, my friend, there is certainly *"nothing new under the sun,"* but when you take heed to the *ProPs* of:

- Salvation • Understanding • Praise • Perseverance • Opportunity • Restoration • Thankfulness

You will be made NEW under the SON!

And when you reach the final page, don't let the journey end—begin it again. The Word of God is living and active, speaking new truths in new seasons. Start back at day one with fresh eyes, a renewed heart, and an eagerness to apply His wisdom in even greater measure. Let this be more than a 365-day devotional; let it be a lifelong pursuit of Christ-centered living.

about the author

Matthew Maher is a 2007 graduate of Temple University, where he earned his Bachelor of Science degree in Business Administration with a concentration in Legal Studies. He is also a former professional soccer player, playing on teams in North Carolina, New Jersey, and Philadelphia respectively. He is the author of the books: *U MAY B THE ONLY BIBLE SOMEBODY READS: R U LEGIBLE?*, *Imprisoned by Peace: A View Apart*, *Unchained: A Voice Apart*, *Let Us Pray: A Plea Apart*, and *Discerning The Devil's Playbook: The Four Plays From Nazi Germany Currently At Play In America* (all available on Amazon.com).

He is the host of the podcast, Rechurched, a podcast aimed at instigating Christians to be Christian, as well as a highly sought-after speaker both on the local and national level. His "Decisions Determine Destiny" program has addressed over 500,000 high school and college students through various events and assemblies.

Matthew is honored to serve as a Pastor at Landmark Church in Ocean City, New Jersey, where his desire is to inspire conscience (so people may know God) and instigate conviction (so people may show God).

You can learn more at www.TruthOverTrend.com, where his blogs have been read by over 1,000,000 people in every state, 121 countries, and in 67 different languages.

Matthew and his beautiful wife, Sarah, along with their daughter, Willow, and sons, Ezekiel and Malachi, reside in Egg Harbor Township, New Jersey.

Social | *@TruthOverTrend*

About the **CORE CONVICTION SERIES**

You have just read Book #4 of the Core Convictions Series. You can find out more information about Book #1, *Imprisoned by Peace*, Book #2, *Unchained*, and Book #3, *Let Us Pray*, by going to TruthOverTrend.com. Please be on the lookout for additional books in this series, as each unique publication looks to embolden the believer's conviction in Christ.

"I'd rather stand alone with Jesus than sit in a crowd without Him." -Matthew Maher

CONNECT WITH
MATTHEW MAHER

@TruthOverTrend

If you are interested in booking Matthew to speak at your next event or would like to check his availability, visit:

TRUTHOVERTREND.COM

Verse-by-verse sermons & studies for you to go deeper in your faith.

thelandmark.church

ALSO AVAILABLE FROM
MATTHEW MAHER

DISCERNING THE DEVIL'S PLAYBOOK
LET US PRAY: A PLEA APART
UNCHAINED: A VOICE APART
IMPRISONED BY PEACE: A VIEW APART
U MAY B THE ONLY BIBLE SOMEBODY READS: R U LEGIBLE?

"Thank you for partnering with us in spreading the Gospel."
Matthew Maher

@TruthOverTrend | *Spreading the truth in a world of trends.*

If you enjoyed this book, will you consider sharing the influence with others?

- Share or mention the book on your social media platforms.

- Encourage your pastor/church to make this resource available to your community.

- Pick up a copy for someone you know who would be spiritually challenged and biblically charged by this message.

- Write a book review on amazon.com.

FOR MORE LITERARY INFLUENCE, PLEASE VISIT:
www.truthovertrend.com/5511-publishing

www.ingramcontent.com/pod-product-compliance
Lightning Source LLC
Chambersburg PA
CBHW070135100426
42743CB00013B/2712